quick & easy

# *after work cookbook*

I dedicate this book to my Mum and Dad with love. You are the best. Also, to my daughter Sophie. Thanks for all your help. Love Mum.

*quick & easy*

# after work cookbook

chrissie taylor

## foulsham

LONDON • NEW YORK • TORONTO • SYDNEY

# foulsham

The Publishing House, Bennetts Close, Cippenham, Berkshire, SL1 5AP, England

ISBN 0-572-02693-5

Cover photograph © The Anthony Blake Photo Library

Printed in Great Britain by The Bath Press, Bath

# Contents

# Introduction

If you are looking for recipes that are simple, quick and easy to prepare and mouth-watering to eat, then this is the book for you. The recipes have been designed to transform everyday, low-cost meals for two into good restaurant-style cuisine with the minimum of fuss, effort and time. Your partner, family and guests will be impressed with the delicious results, which even the novice cook can prepare without expert cooking skills.

The variety of new products – some fresh, others designed for convenience – increases as our taste for more exotic and unusual flavours expands. We can harness these innovations to make our cooking more interesting and enjoyable. No one wants to work hard all day and then have to spend hours in the kitchen preparing a meal, but we all want to eat well. With these recipes that's not a problem!

Many of the recipes in this book are created from cupboard and freezer favourites, so once you have set up a basic storecupboard, you don't need special shopping trips.

To make them as convenient as possible, the recipes have been calculated for two people, but they can easily be halved or doubled to suit your requirements. I've also included plenty of recipes for vegetarians or near-vegetarians, as so many people are cutting down on the amount of red meat, in particular, in their diet. If you are following a low-fat or sugar-free diet, you can easily make appropriate substitutions.

Remember that presentation is important, even at the end of a hard day at work. I've given ideas for garnishes so that you really make the most of your food and enjoy the eating experience.

The recipes in this book use short-cut cookery to suit every lifestyle and you can use them as TV snacks and suppers or serve them to friends at a dinner party with minimum effort and time. I hope you will enjoy sharing them with me.

# Your After Work Storecupboard

A well-stocked and organised storecupboard is invaluable in any kitchen if you want to prepare and cook dishes quickly and easily.

The range of foods that can now be bought and stored is vast and, with the benefit of modern packaging and the use of home freezers, many of the ingredients used in this book will be ready to hand.

The following is a comprehensive list of the ingredients that I consider should be in your storecupboard and freezer to assist you in making the recipes in this book.

## Jars, Bottles and Cans

Antipasto and wild mushrooms
Canned tomatoes
Tomato juice
Sun-dried tomatoes
Sieved tomatoes (passata)
Olives: black, green
Oils: sesame, olive, vegetable, stir-fry

Tuna fish
Sweetcorn (corn)
Peanut butter
Sun-ripened tomato and basil sauce
Fruity hot jalfrezi sauce
Bourgignonne sauce
Mango chutney
Kidney beans
White wine and garlic cooking sauce
Alcohol: brandy, dry cider, Cointreau, milk stout, port, sherry, whisky, white wine
Mayonnaise
Chickpeas (garbanzos)
Apricot halves
Pineapple pieces

## Fridge and Freezer

Pastry (paste): filo, puff, shortcrust (basic pie crust)
Milk
Cheese: Cheddar, Mascapone, Mozzarella, Parmesan
Butter, including unsalted (sweet)
Low-fat spread
Natural yoghurt
Cream: single (light), double (heavy)
Prawns (shrimp)
Smoked salmon
Unsweetened orange juice
Eggs
Mangetout (snow peas)
Vanilla ice cream

# Dried and Other Essentials

Flour: plain (all-purpose), self-raising (self-rising), granary, cornflour (cornstarch)
Parsley sauce
Nuts: salted peanuts, pine nuts, almonds, cashews, pistachios
Rice: basmati, long-grain, brown, wild
Pasta: tagliatelle, spaghetti, shapes
Egg noodles
Arrowroot
Couscous
Baking powder
Breads: melba toast, croûtons, rolls, flour tortillas, pitta breads, ciabattas, French sticks

# Sweet Standbys

Honey: clear, set
Sugar: soft brown, caster (superfine), icing (confectioners')
Jam (jelly): plum, apricot
Apple sauce
Dried apricots
Raisins
Sultanas (golden raisins)
Spreads: chocolate, vanilla
Chocolate: white, milk (sweet), plain (semi-sweet)
Ready-to-serve custard
Digestive biscuits (graham crackers)
Lemon curd
Meringue nests
Shortbread fingers
Drinking chocolate (sweetened chocolate) powder

# Flavour Enhancers

Fresh or freeze-dried herbs: basil, chives, coriander (cilantro), dill (dill weed), mint, oregano, parsley, rosemary, tarragon, thyme

Dried herbs: herbes de Provence, mixed herbs, thyme

Spices: cayenne, chilli, cinnamon, cloves, cumin, garam masala, ground ginger, nutmeg, paprika, whole black peppercorns, tandoori paste, Thai red curry paste, vanilla pods

Salt

Garlic purée (paste)

Tomato purée, including sun-dried

Mustard: Dijon, English, French, wholegrain

Vinegar: balsamic, cider, malt, red wine, white wine

Stock cubes: chicken, beef, vegetable, stir-fry

Gravy powder or granules

Curry paste or powder

Lemon juice

Pesto and pesto sauce

Seeds: sesame, pumpkin, sunflower

Tomato ketchup (catsup)

Anchovy fillets and paste

Capers

Pickles: brown, lime

Vanilla essence (extract)

Instant coffee powder or granules

# Notes on the Recipes

* Do not mix metric, imperial and American measures. Follow one set only.

* All spoon measures are level: 1 tsp = 5 ml;
                                  1 tbsp = 15 ml.

* Eggs are medium unless otherwise stated.

* Always wash, peel, core and seed, if necessary, fresh fruit and vegetables before use. Ensure that all food is as fresh as possible and in good condition. Clean all meat and fish appropriately before cooking.

* Use fresh herbs where possible, but if it is necessary to use dried use half the amount stated. Chopped frozen varieties are better than dried. There is no substitute for fresh parsley and coriander (cilantro). Many varieties of herbs and garlic can now be bought ready prepared in jars.

* Can and packet sizes are approximate.

* Use your own discretion in substituting ingredients and personalising the recipes.

* Use kitchen gadgets to speed up preparation and cooking times: mixers for whisking; food processors for chopping, grating, slicing and mixing; blenders for liquidising.

* Always preheat the oven and cook on the centre shelf unless otherwise specified or using a fan-assisted oven.

* Times include both preparation and cooking.

* All ovens vary, so cooking times have to be approximate. Adjust cooking times and temperatures to suit your own appliance, especially if you have a fan-assisted oven.

* Cream or yoghurt or a mixture of the two can be substituted for crème fraîche. Crème fraîche should not be allowed to boil.

* Some recipes contain nuts. Traditional pesto contains pine nuts, so check with the manufacturer's list of ingredients if you buy it ready prepared. To achieve a similar flavour without nuts, place a small handful of basil leaves, some grated Parmesan cheese and olive oil into a blender and mix to a smooth paste.

# Soups and Starters

The soups and starters in this book are quick and easy to prepare and also very versatile. They can be served as a starter to a three-course meal, as a snack, for supper or they can make a delicious light meal with crusty bread followed by fresh fruit or a cheese-board.

The ideas I have given for their final presentation can turn an everyday dish into part of a memorable meal.

# Creamy Carrot and Orange Soup

**Serves 2**

225 g/8 oz carrots, roughly chopped
1 small onion, roughly chopped
150 ml/¼ pt/⅔ cup milk
150 ml/¼ pt/⅔ cup chicken stock
Salt and freshly ground black pepper
Grated rind and juice of ½ orange
15 ml/1 tbsp chopped parsley
30 ml/2 tbsp crème fraîche

1 Place the carrots, onion, milk and stock in a saucepan. Season to taste. Bring to the boil, cover and simmer for about 15 minutes until tender.

2 Purée in a food processor or blender or rub through a sieve (strainer).

3 Return to the saucepan, stir in the orange rind and juice and reheat gently but do not allow to boil. Taste and re-season, if necessary.

4 Serve hot or cold, garnished with the parsley and a swirl of crème fraîche.

🕐 **25 minutes**

✱ If you are reheating the soup, do not add the orange rind or juice until serving or it may curdle.

# Cheesy Potato Chowder

**Serves 2**
15 ml/1 tbsp vegetable oil
1 small red onion, chopped
2.5 ml/½ tsp garlic purée (paste)
25 g/1 oz/¼ cup plain (all-purpose) flour
450 ml/3/4 pt/2 cups hot vegetable stock
2 potatoes, peeled and cut into large dice
Salt and freshly ground black pepper
150 ml/¼ pt/⅔ cup milk
100 g/4 oz/1 cup Red Leicester cheese, diced
15 ml/1 tbsp chopped parsley
Crusty bread, to serve

1 Heat the oil in a flameproof casserole dish (Dutch oven) and cook the onion and garlic purée for 2 minutes until softened but not browned.

2 Stir in the flour and cook for 1 minute. Gradually add the stock and mix until smooth, then bring to the boil.

3 Stir in the potatoes and season with salt and pepper.

4 Cover and cook in a preheated oven at 150°C/300°F/gas mark 2 for 20–25 minutes until the potatoes are tender.

5 Just before serving, stir in the milk, cheese and parsley and re-season, if necessary. Serve with chunks of fresh crusty bread.

⏱ 40 minutes

✳ You can use a mature Cheddar or similar hard cheese instead of Red Leicester, if you prefer, and add some diced cooked bacon or ham for a more substantial soup.

# Tomato Chilli Soup

**Serves 2**

1 vegetable stock cube
30 ml/2 tbsp water
500 ml/17 fl oz/2¼ cups tomato juice
5 ml/1 tsp garlic purée (paste)
5 ml/1 tsp chilli paste
15 ml/1 tbsp chopped basil or chives
Salt and freshly ground black pepper
30 ml/2 tbsp plain yoghurt or fromage frais
Crusty bread, to serve

1 Place the stock cube in a saucepan with the water and heat until it dissolves.

2 Add the tomato juice, garlic purée and chilli paste and bring to the boil.

3 Reserve 5 ml/1 tsp of the herbs for garnish, then add the rest to the pan and season with salt and pepper.

4 Ladle into soup bowls and add a spoonful of yoghurt or fromage frais to each. Sprinkle with the reserved herbs and a little ground black pepper and serve with crusty bread.

## 15 minutes

✳ Add some cooked pasta shapes at the last minute for a more substantial soup.

# Farmhouse Turkey Tureen

**Serves 2**
25 g/1 oz/2 tbsp butter or margarine
25 g/1 oz/¼ cup plain (all-purpose) flour
350 ml/12 fl oz/1⅓ cups vegetable stock
2 small carrots, thinly sliced
6 cherry tomatoes, halved
2.5 ml/½ tsp dried thyme
100 g/4 oz mushrooms, sliced
225 g/8 oz/2 cups cooked turkey, diced
Salt and freshly ground black pepper
10 ml/2 tsp chopped parsley
Crusty farmhouse bread, to serve

1 Melt the butter or margarine, stir in the flour and cook for 1 minute.

2 Gradually add the stock and bring to the boil, stirring, to make a smooth sauce.

3 Add the carrots, tomatoes and thyme, then cover and simmer for 5 minutes.

4 Add the mushrooms and turkey, cover and simmer for a further 5 minutes.

5 Season to taste with salt and pepper, sprinkle with the parsley and serve with wedges of fresh crusty farmhouse bread.

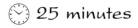 25 minutes

# Iced Avocado Soup

**Serves 2**

1 ripe avocado, peeled, halved and stoned (pitted)
45 ml/3 tbsp lemon juice
10 ml/2 tsp snipped chives
350 ml/12 fl oz/1⅓ cups chicken stock, chilled
45 ml/3 tbsp plain yoghurt
Salt and freshly ground black pepper
30 ml/2 tbsp single (light) or soured (dairy sour) cream
Melba toast or mini croûtons, to serve

1 Place the avocado, lemon juice, chives and stock in a food processor and process until blended.

2 Add the yoghurt, season generously with salt and pepper and process again until smooth.

3 Spoon into bowls and chill.

4 Add a swirl of cream into the centre of each bowl and serve with melba toast or mini croûtons.

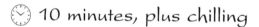 10 minutes, plus chilling

# Baked Camembert with Sun-dried Tomato Chutney

**Serves 2**

150 g/5 oz Camembert (in a box)
1 garlic clove, halved
45 ml/3 tbsp white wine
*For the sun-dried tomato chutney:*
30 ml/2 tbsp white wine
50 g/2 oz sun-dried tomatoes, chopped
15 ml/1 tbsp white wine vinegar
10 ml/2 tsp tomato purée (paste)
15 ml/1 tbsp light brown sugar
10 ml/2 tsp roughly chopped fresh basil
Melba toast, to serve

1  Remove the paper wrapping from the Camembert and replace the cheese in the box. Pierce the top of cheese a few times with a fork and rub the surface with the garlic.

2  Drizzle 15 ml/1 tbsp of the wine over, replace the lid on the box and place on a baking (cookie) sheet.

3  Cook in a preheated oven at 220°C/425°F/gas mark 7 for 5–6 minutes until heated through and soft.

4  Meanwhile, to make the chutney, place the remaining wine and all the other ingredients except the basil in a saucepan. Bring to the boil, stirring constantly, then simmer uncovered for 3–4 minutes until thickened.

5  Stir in the basil and serve with the cheese and melba toast.

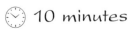 10 minutes

# Avocado with Peanut Dressing

**Serves 2**

1 medium avocado, halved and stoned (pitted)
5 ml/1 tsp lemon juice
*For the dressing:*
10 ml/2 tsp salted peanuts, finely chopped
5 ml/1 tsp clear honey
5 ml/1 tsp lemon juice
5 ml/1 tsp sesame oil
Salt and freshly ground black pepper

1   Place the avocado halves in a serving dish and sprinkle with the lemon juice to prevent browning.

2   To make the dressing, place all the ingredients in a bowl or screw-topped jar and whisk or shake well.

3   Pour into the centre of the avocado halves and serve immediately.

🕐 10 minutes

# Chicken Liver and Cream Cheese Pâté

**Serves 2**
5 ml/1 tsp olive oil
100 g/4 oz chicken livers
7.5 ml/1½ tsp sun-dried tomato purée (paste)
50 g/2 oz/¼ cup garlic and herb cream cheese
Salt and freshly ground black pepper
Parsley sprigs and lemon wedges, to garnish
French bread or melba toast, to serve

1 Heat the oil and fry (sauté) the chicken livers over a medium heat for 4–5 minutes, turning occasionally.

2 Stir in the tomato purée and leave to cool.

3 Place in a food blender with the cheese and seasoning and process until smooth.

4 Divide between two ramekins (custard cups) and chill. Garnish with parsley sprigs and lemon wedges and serve with French bread or melba toast.

🕑 10 minutes, plus chilling

# Prawn and Cream Cheese Pâté

**Serves 2**

75 g/3 oz/⅓ cup soft cream cheese
2 spring onions (scallions), finely chopped
100 g/4 oz cooked, peeled prawns (shrimp), chopped
15 ml/1 tbsp lemon juice
10 ml/2 tsp chopped dill (dill weed)
Salt and freshly ground black pepper
4 whole prawns
2 dill sprigs
Crusty bread or melba toast, to serve

1  Place the cheese in a bowl, add the spring onions, chopped prawns, lemon juice and chopped dill and season to taste. Mix well until smooth.

2  Divide between two ramekins (custard cups) and smooth the tops. Chill.

3  Garnish with the whole prawns and dill sprigs and serve with crusty bread or melba toast.

🕐 10 minutes, plus chilling

# Crab and Sweetcorn Melts

### Serves 2

5 ml/1 tsp olive oil
2 spring onions (scallions), finely chopped
5 ml/1 tsp crushed garlic
A pinch of chilli powder
175 ml/6 fl oz/¾ cup ready-made parsley sauce
175 g/6 oz/1 small can of crabmeat, drained
50 g/2 oz canned or frozen sweetcorn (corn)
Salt and freshly ground black pepper
50 g/2 oz/½ cup Gruyère (Swiss) cheese, grated
Melba toast, to serve

1  Heat the oil and fry (sauté) the onions, garlic and chilli powder for 2 minutes.

2  Transfer to a bowl and mix in the parsley sauce, crabmeat and sweetcorn and season with salt and pepper.

3  Divide between two ramekins (custard cups) and sprinkle with the cheese.

4  Cook in a preheated oven at 200°C/400°F/gas mark 6 for 15 minutes until heated through and the cheese has melted. Serve immediately with melba toast.

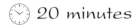 20 minutes

# Napoli Stacks

**Serves 2**

3 plum tomatoes, sliced
150 g/5 oz Mozzarella cheese, sliced
2 spring onions (scallions), finely sliced
12 black olives, stoned (pitted)
*For the dressing:*
30 ml/2 tbsp olive oil
5 ml/1 tsp crushed garlic
15 ml/1 tbsp balsamic vinegar
15 ml/1 tbsp chopped basil
Salt and freshly ground black pepper

1  Arrange layers of tomato and cheese slices and onions on two plates and scatter the olives over the top.

2  To make the dressing, place all the ingredients in a bowl or screw-topped jar and whisk or shake well. Pour over the Napoli stacks and chill before serving.

🕐 10 minutes, plus chilling

# Strawberry and Avocado Salad

**Serves 2**

1 ripe avocado, peeled, halved and stoned (pitted)
10 ml/2 tsp lemon juice
100 g/4 oz fresh strawberries, hulled and quartered
5 cm/2 in piece of cucumber, peeled and sliced
50 g/2 oz/1 bag of Italian-style salad
45 ml/3 tbsp unsweetened orange juice
15 ml/1 tbsp balsamic vinegar
Freshly ground black pepper

1　Cut the avocado into bite-sized pieces and toss in the lemon juice. Mix in the strawberries and cucumber.

2　Reserve a few salad leaves and put the remainder in a salad bowl. Place the strawberry and avocado mixture on top of the leaves.

3　Mix together the orange juice and vinegar and add pepper to taste. Pour over the salad, add the reserved leaves and toss carefully.

🕐 10 minutes

✳ This salad can also be served as an accompaniment to cold meat.

# Seafood Dishes

Fish is naturally very quick and easy to cook, which makes it an invaluable inclusion in this book. Some of the recipes include diary products, so adjust the ingredients accordingly to suit your dietary regime, especially if vegetarian.

# Baked Mackerel in White Wine with Fennel

**Serves 2**
15 ml/1 tbsp olive oil
1 large fennel bulb, trimmed, sliced and blanched
2.5 ml/½ tsp chopped garlic
2 mackerel, washed and heads removed
45 ml/3 tbsp white wine
Salt and freshly ground black pepper
½ lemon, sliced
New potatoes and fresh vegetables, to serve

1 Grease the bottom of an ovenproof dish with half the oil. Lay the fennel leaves on the base, scatter with the garlic and lay the mackerel on top.

2 Pour the wine over, season with salt and pepper and lay the lemon slices on top. Drizzle with the remaining oil and cover with foil.

3 Bake on the top shelf of a preheated oven at 200°C/400°F/gas mark 6 for 10 minutes.

4 Remove the foil and increase the temperature to 230°C/450°F/gas mark 8 and cook for a further 10–15 minutes until the lemon slices are golden brown and the fish skin is crisp and golden.

5 Serve with new potatoes and fresh vegetables.

## 🕑 30 minutes

✳ For a variation, substitute 15 ml/1 tbsp Pernod for the wine.

# Lime and Tarragon Tuna

**Serves 2**

2 tuna steaks
*For the marinade:*
30 ml/2 tbsp olive oil
15 ml/1 tbsp clear honey
5 ml/1 tsp grated root ginger
15 ml/1 tbsp chopped tarragon
Grated rind and juice of ½ lime
Salt and fresh ground black pepper
Mixed leaf salad and cherry tomatoes, to serve

1 Wash the tuna steaks, pat them dry on kitchen paper (paper towels) and lay the fish in a non-metallic dish.

2 Mix together the marinade ingredients, pour over the tuna steaks, cover and chill for 2 hours.

3 Bake in a preheated oven at 200°C/400°F/gas mark 6 for 18–20 minutes.

4 Serve with a crisp mixed leaf salad and cherry tomatoes.

🕧 *30 minutes, plus chilling*

# Grilled Salmon with Watercress Sauce

**Serves 2**
2 salmon fillets
*For the marinade:*
30 ml/2 tbsp balsamic vinegar
15 ml/1 tbsp olive oil
15 ml/1 tbsp lemon juice
10 ml/2 tsp chopped thyme
Salt and freshly ground black pepper
*For the watercress sauce:*
50 g/2 oz watercress, chopped
120 ml/4 fl oz/½ cup crème fraîche
2.5 ml/½ tsp French mustard
10 ml/2 tsp lemon juice
Tomato and onion salad and new potatoes, to serve

1 Place the salmon fillets in a non-metallic dish.

2 Mix together the marinade ingredients and pour over the fish. Cover and chill for 1 hour.

3 Place the watercress, crème fraîche and mustard in a pan and heat gently, stirring. Add the lemon juice and season.

4 Lift the salmon from the marinade and transfer to a preheated grill (broiler). Grill (broil) for 3–4 minutes each side, brushing frequently with the marinade.

5 Pour the sauce over and serve with a tomato and onion salad and new potatoes.

🕑 15 minutes, plus marinating

✶ For a more intense flavour, marinate in the fridge overnight.

# Salmon Steaks with Pesto and Pine Nuts

### Serves 2

2 salmon steaks
Salt and freshly ground black pepper
25 g/1 oz/2 tbsp butter or margarine
50 g/2 oz/1 cup fresh white breadcrumbs
30 ml/2 tbsp green pesto sauce with whole pine nuts
10 ml/2 tsp finely grated lemon rind
1 small egg, beaten
Rocket leaves, dill (dill weed) sprigs and lemon slices, to serve

1   Wash the salmon in cold water and pat dry on kitchen paper (paper towels). Season generously with pepper.

2   Melt the butter or margarine in a pan and add the breadcrumbs. Toss until browned, then leave to cool.

3   Place the pesto, lemon rind and breadcrumbs in a bowl and season with salt. Mix until combined.

4   Dip the salmon in the egg and place in an ovenproof dish. Spoon the breadcrumb mixture on top of the steaks, pressing down gently.

5   Bake in a preheated oven at 200°C/400°F/gas mark 6 for 10–15 minutes until the topping is golden brown.

6   Serve on a bed of rocket leaves with dill sprigs and lemon slices and any cooking juices.

## ⏲ 25 minutes

✸   For a nut-free pesto, see page 13.

# Parma-wrapped Salmon with Pesto Mash

**Serves 2**

450 g/1 lb potatoes, peeled, washed and cubed
2 slices of Parma ham
2 salmon fillets
Freshly ground black pepper
60 ml/4 tbsp single (light) cream
60 ml/4 tbsp fresh green pesto sauce
30 ml/2 tbsp olive oil
Roasted vine tomatoes, to serve

1   Cook the potatoes in boiling salted water for 15–20 minutes.

2   Meanwhile, line a baking (cookie) sheet with foil and lay the Parma ham on top. Place a salmon fillet on each piece, sprinkle some pepper over and wrap the ham around the salmon.

3   Bake in a preheated oven at 190°C/375°F/gas mark 5 for 8–10 minutes until just cooked.

4   Drain the potatoes and mash in the cream. Reserve 15 ml/ 1 tbsp of the pesto and mash the remainder into the potato. Reheat gently, stirring to prevent burning.

5   Divide the pesto mash between two warm plates and top each with a salmon parcel.

6   Mix together the reserved pesto and the oil and drizzle over each parcel. Serve with roasted vine tomatoes.

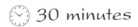 30 minutes

✻ This recipe also works well with chicken breasts or pork fillets instead of salmon, though the baking time should be increased to 25–30 minutes until the meat is tender and cooked through. For a nut-free pesto, see page 13.

# Thatched Cod Bake

**Serves 2**
45 ml/3 tbsp fresh white breadcrumbs
25 g/1 oz/¼ cup Cheddar cheese, grated
15 ml/1 tbsp chopped parsley
4 sun-dried tomatoes in oil, drained and chopped
Salt and freshly ground black pepper
30 ml/2 tbsp oil from the tomatoes
2 cod fillets, about 100 g/4 oz each
Mixed salad or new potatoes and vegetables, to serve

1 Place the breadcrumbs, cheese, parsley, tomatoes, salt and pepper and half the oil in a bowl and mix to combine.

2 Place the cod in a shallow ovenproof dish and top with the breadcrumb mixture.

3 Drizzle the remaining oil over and bake in a preheated oven at 200°C/400°F/gas mark 6 for 10–15 minutes until the cod is flaking and the topping is golden.

4 Serve with a mixed salad or new potatoes and vegetables.

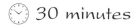 30 minutes

# Griddled Swordfish with Tomato Salsa

**Serves 2**

25 ml/1½ tbsp olive oil
1 small onion, finely chopped
2.5 ml/½ tsp chilli paste
225 g/8 oz/1 small can of chopped tomatoes
15 ml/1 tbsp tomato purée (paste)
Salt and freshly ground black pepper
2 swordfish steaks, about 100 g/4 oz each
2 rosemary sprigs, to garnish
Buttered new potatoes and baby sweetcorn (corn), to serve

1   Heat 15 ml/1 tbsp of the oil and fry (sauté) the onion for 3–4 minutes until softened.

2   Add the chilli paste, tomatoes and tomato purée. Stir well and simmer, uncovered, for 15–20 minutes until the sauce has thickened and reduced slightly. Season to taste with salt and pepper.

3   Heat the remaining oil on a griddle or in a frying pan (skillet). Season the steaks with salt and pepper and cook for 3 minutes on each side.

4   Spoon the salsa sauce over the steaks, garnish each with a sprig of rosemary and serve with buttered new potatoes and baby sweetcorn.

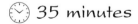 35 minutes

# Pesto Baked Cod

### Serves 2

2 cod fillets, about 100 g/4 oz each
10 ml/2 tsp lemon juice
Salt and freshly ground black pepper
30 ml/2 tbsp pesto sauce
45 ml/3 tbsp fresh white breadcrumbs
25 g/1 oz/¼ cup Procaine cheese, finely grated
New potatoes and baby carrots, to serve

1   Place the cod in a baking dish and sprinkle with the lemon juice. Season with salt and pepper.

2   Mix the pesto with 30 ml/2 tbsp of the breadcrumbs to form a paste. Spread evenly over the top of the fish.

3   Mix the remaining breadcrumbs with half the cheese and sprinkle over the pesto paste. Top with the remaining cheese.

4   Bake in a preheated oven at 230ºC/450ºF/gas mark 8 for 10 minutes until the cod is just cooked and the topping is crisp and golden brown.

5   Serve with new potatoes and baby carrots.

### 🕐 25 minutes

✴  This recipe is equally good with haddock or salmon. For a nut-free pesto, see page 13.

# Cod and Prawn Tempura

**Serves 2**

1 small egg yolk
150 ml/¼ pt/⅔ cup ice-cold water
75 g/3 oz/¾ cup plain (all-purpose) flour
175 g/6 oz cod fillet, cut into bite-sized cubes
100 g/4 oz prawns (shrimp), peeled, thawed and drained if frozen
Oil, for deep-frying
Sweet chilli sauce or sweet and sour sauce, boiled rice and prawn crackers, to serve

1   Place the egg yolk and water in bowl and whisk together. Stir in 50 g/2 oz/½ cup of the flour and beat until smooth.

2   Dip the cod pieces and prawns in the remaining flour.

3   Heat the oil to 190°C/375°F or until a cube of day-old bread browns in 10–15 seconds.

4   Place the cod pieces and prawns on a slotted spoon, dip in the batter and drain off the excess.

5   Fry (sauté) the cod pieces for 2–3 minutes and the prawns for 1–2 minutes until crisp and golden brown. Drain on kitchen paper (paper towels).

6   Serve immediately with a sweet chilli sauce dip or sweet and sour sauce and boiled rice and prawn crackers.

⏱ 20 minutes

✴  The batter in this recipe is deliciously crisp and light. Make sure the cooking oil is hot enough so that the tempura stay crisp.

# Thai-style Prawns

## Serves 2

10 ml/2 tsp sesame oil
5 ml/1 tsp chopped garlic
10 ml/2 tsp grated root ginger
30 ml/2 tbsp chopped coriander (cilantro)
5–10 ml/1–2 tsp chilli paste, to taste
30 ml/2 tbsp soy sauce
225 g/8 oz prawns (shrimp), peeled, thawed and
drained if frozen
Plain boiled rice, to serve

1   Mix together all the ingredients except the prawns in a heatproof bowl.

2   Add the prawns and toss well.

3   Place the bowl in a steamer or over a pan of simmering water. Cover and steam for 8–10 minutes until the prawns are hot and cooked through.

4   Serve immediately with boiled rice.

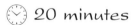 20 minutes

# Coconut Prawns

**Serves 2**

10 ml/2 tsp sesame oil
4 spring onions (scallions), chopped
100 ml/3½ fl oz/scant ½ cup creamed coconut
100 ml/3½ fl oz/scant ½ cup water
1 fish stock cube
15 ml/1 tbsp Thai red curry paste
275 g/10 oz large prawns (jumbo shrimp), thawed if frozen
and shelled
15 ml/1 tbsp chopped coriander (cilantro)
Salt and freshly ground black pepper
Savoury rice, to serve

1   Heat the oil in a wok or frying pan (skillet), add the spring
    onions and stir-fry for 2–3 minutes to soften.

2   Add the creamed coconut, water, stock cube and curry
    paste and bring to the boil.

3   Add the prawns and cook over a moderate heat for
    5–6 minutes.

4   Add 10 ml/2 tsp of the coriander and season to taste with
    salt and pepper.

5   Serve on a bed of savoury rice and garnish with the
    remaining coriander.

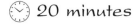 20 minutes

# Garlic and Ginger King Prawns with Bacon

### Serves 2

30 ml/2 tbsp lime juice

2.5 ml/½ tsp crushed garlic

2.5 ml/½ tsp grated root ginger

5 ml/1 tsp soft brown sugar

16 uncooked king prawns (jumbo shrimp), peeled and veins removed

8 streaky bacon rashers (slices), rinded and halved

Lime wedges, to garnish

Green salad leaves and cherry tomatoes, to serve

1   Place the lime juice, garlic, ginger and sugar in a bowl and mix well. Add the prawns and toss to coat. Cover and chill for 30 minutes.

2   Wrap a piece of bacon round each prawn and thread two each on small skewers.

3   Cook under a medium grill (broiler) for 2 minutes each side, basting with any remaining marinade.

4   Garnish with lime wedges and serve immediately with crisp green salad leaves and cherry tomatoes.

⏲ 15 minutes, plus chilling

# Prawn and Ginger Chilli Fritters

**Serves 2**

1 slice of white bread, crusts removed
100 g/4 oz uncooked, peeled prawns (shrimp)
2.5 ml/½ tsp chopped green chilli
5 ml/1 tsp grated root ginger
5 ml/1 tsp chopped coriander (cilantro)
Salt and freshly ground black pepper
½ small egg, beaten
Vegetable oil, for shallow-frying
Baby lettuce leaves, to serve
Lime or lemon wedges, to garnish

1   Place the bread in a bowl and cover with water. Soak for about 10 seconds, then squeeze out the water.

2   Place the bread in a food processor with the remaining ingredients and process for a few seconds until blended but not smooth.

3   Pour the oil into a pan to a depth of 2.5 cm/1 in and fry (sauté) spoonfuls of the prawn mixture for 2 minutes on each side until puffed up and golden brown.

4   Drain on kitchen paper (paper towels), arrange on a bed of baby lettuce leaves and serve immediately, garnished with lime or lemon wedges.

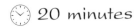 20 minutes

# Prawn Salsa Pittas

**Serves 2**

100 g/4 oz/1 small packet of smoked king prawns (jumbo shrimp), thawed and peeled
1 small red onion, finely chopped
1 tomato, finely chopped
15 ml/1 tbsp chopped coriander (cilantro)
1 lime
15 ml/1 tbsp olive oil
2.5 ml/½ tsp caster (superfine) sugar
2.5 ml/½ tsp chilli paste
10 ml/2 tsp sun-dried tomato purée (paste)
Freshly ground black pepper
4 mini pitta breads

1   Place the prawns in a bowl with the onion and tomato and all but 5 ml/1 tsp of the coriander. Toss well.

2   Halve the lime lengthways and cut one half into wedges for garnish.

3   Squeeze the juice from the other lime half and mix well with the oil, sugar, chilli paste and tomato purée. Pour over the prawn mixture and season with pepper. Toss well to combine.

4   Grill (broil) the pitta breads, place on a serving plate and top with the prawn salsa. Garnish with the remaining coriander and the lime wedges and serve.

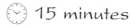 15 minutes

# Smoked Salmon and Wild Mushroom Tagliatelle

**Serves 2**

175 g/6 oz tagliatelle
50 g/2 oz smoked salmon pieces
100 g/4 oz/1 small jar of antipasto wild mushrooms,
drained and chopped
60 ml/4 tbsp red pesto sauce
15 ml/1 tbsp chopped parsley
Freshly ground black pepper
Garlic bread, to serve

1  Cook the tagliatelle in boiling salted water for about 10 minutes until just tender. Drain well, then return to the hot pan.

2  Add the salmon, mushrooms and pesto and toss together.

3  Reheat gently, add the parsley and season with pepper, then toss again to combine.

4  Serve immediately with garlic bread.

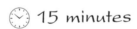 15 minutes

✷  For a nut-free pesto, see page 13.

# Vegetarian Dishes

A note for the most committed of carnivores – don't be afraid to go vegetarian for a change. Many people are now reducing the amount of meat they eat and we need to reinforce the fact that a meat-free diet can be as healthy and nourishing as one that includes meat. A well-balanced vegetarian meal is now widely regarded as the healthiest choice for your diet. However, when cooking for serious vegetarians, make sure that all the ingredients, especially cheese and diary products, are suitable.

# Vegetarian Risotto

**Serves 2**

50 g/2 oz Parmesan cheese
450 ml/¾ pt/2 cups hot vegetable stock
15 ml/1 tbsp olive oil
1 small onion, peeled and finely chopped
5 ml/1 tsp chopped garlic
150 g/5 oz/⅔ cup risotto rice
100 ml/3½ fl oz/scant ½ cup dry white wine
50 g/2 oz chestnut mushrooms, quartered
½ red (bell) pepper, seeded and sliced
Salt and freshly ground black pepper
75 g/3 oz canned asparagus, drained
and cut into 5 cm/2 in pieces
25 g/1 oz/2 tbsp butter or margarine

1 Using a potato peeler, shave a few slithers from the Parmesan and reserve for garnish. Grate the remainder.

2 Keep the vegetable stock at simmering point while making the risotto. Heat the oil in a pan and fry (sauté) the onion gently for 2–3 minutes until soft. Add the garlic and cook for a further 1 minute.

3 Add the rice, increase the heat and cook, stirring constantly, until the rice is opaque. Add the wine and stir until it has been absorbed.

4 Add a quarter of the stock, reduce the heat and stir until the stock is absorbed. Repeat until all the rice is tender but still has some 'bite', adding the mushrooms and red pepper with the final addition of stock. Keep stirring so the stock is evenly absorbed and does not stick. (You may not need to use all the stock as the absorbency of ristotto rice varies.) Season to taste.

5   Stir in the asparagus and heat through. Remove from the heat, add the butter or margarine and the grated Parmesan. Stir, cover with lid and leave to stand for 2–3 minutes.

6   Serve sprinkled with the Parmesan slivers and a grinding of black pepper.

🕐 30 minutes

# Roasted Tomato and Feta Tagliatelle

**Serves 2**

450 g/1 lb tomatoes, cut into 1 cm/½ in pieces
5 ml/1 tsp crushed garlic
60 ml/4 tbsp olive oil
175 g/6 oz tagliatelle
100 g/4 oz Feta cheese, cut into 1 cm/½ in cubes
10 ml/2 tsp chopped basil
Salt and freshly ground black pepper
Torn basil leaves, to garnish

1   Place the tomatoes in a shallow baking tray. Mix together the garlic and oil, drizzle over the tomatoes and roast in a preheated oven at 200°C/400°F/gas mark 6 for 30 minutes.

2   Cook the tagliatelle according to the packet directions. Drain, return to the saucepan and add the roasted tomatoes with their juices, the cheese and basil.

3   Season to taste and serve immediately, garnished with a few torn basil leaves.

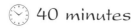 40 minutes

# Roasted Stuffed Peppers

**Serves 2**

2 large red, green or yellow (bell) peppers
15 ml/1 tbsp olive oil
1 onion, thinly sliced
2 small courgettes (zucchini), diced
2.5 ml/½ tsp garlic purée (paste)
15 ml/1 tbsp pine nuts
6 cherry tomatoes, halved
4 black olives, stoned (pitted) and chopped
15 ml/1 tbsp chopped basil or oregano
25 g/1 oz couscous, soaked in vegetable stock according
to the packet directions
Salt and freshly ground black pepper
Crusty bread and a crisp green salad, to serve

1 Slice the tops from the peppers and reserve. Scoop out the seeds and brush the outer skins and tops with oil. Place on a baking (cookie) sheet.

2 Fry (sauté) the onion and courgettes in the remaining oil for 3–4 minutes to soften. Remove from the heat and stir in the remaining ingredients.

3 Fill the peppers with the mixture, replace the tops and bake in a preheated oven at 220°C/425°F/gas mark 7 for 15–20 minutes until the peppers are soft and the filling is heated through.

4 Serve with crusty bread and a crisp green salad.

 40 minutes

# Mushroom and Herb Melts

**Serves 2**

175 g/6 oz frozen puff pastry (paste), thawed
15 ml/1 tbsp olive oil
100 g/4 oz oyster mushrooms, sliced
100 g/4 oz chestnut mushrooms, sliced
7.5 ml/1½ tsp grated garlic
90 ml/6 tbsp crème fraîche
2.5 ml/½ tsp chopped thyme or oregano
Salt and freshly ground black pepper
Buttered new potatoes and mangetout (snow peas), to serve

1   Roll out the pastry to 5 mm/¼ in thick and cut two 13 cm/5 in diameter rounds. Place on a baking tray and bake in a preheated oven at 230°C/450°F/gas mark 8 for 8–10 minutes until puffed up and golden.

2   Heat half the oil and fry (sauté) the oyster mushrooms for 2 minutes. Add the chestnut mushrooms and fry for 2 minutes. Remove with a slotted spoon and keep warm.

3   Boil the juices until reduced by half, then return the mushrooms to pan with the garlic, crème fraîche, herbs and seasoning. Heat, but do not allow to boil.

4   Split the pastry rounds in half and fill each base with the mushroom mixture. Cover with the tops and serve with buttered new potatoes and mangetout.

## ⊙ 30 minutes

✱   If you wish, you can prepare the pastry cases (pie shells) in advance, then reheat them in the oven.

# Double Mushroom Galettes

**Serves 2**

50 g/2 oz cold mashed potato
100 g/4 oz/1 cup self-raising (self-rising) flour
Salt and freshly ground black pepper
40 g/1½ oz/3 tbsp butter or margarine
*For the double mushroom topping:*
7.5 ml/1½ tsp olive oil
1 red onion, cut into wedges
50 g/2 oz shiitake mushrooms, halved
100 g/4 oz baby button mushrooms
2.5 ml/½ tsp chopped garlic
4 sun-dried tomatoes in oil, sliced
15 g/½ oz/2 tbsp pine nuts or cashew nuts, toasted
5 ml/1 tsp chopped parsley
10 ml/2 tsp mushroom ketchup (catsup)
30 ml/2 tbsp Mascarpone cheese
Mixed salad, to serve

1 Place the potato, flour and seasoning in a bowl and mix to combine. Rub in the butter or margarine until the mixture forms a dough.

2 Halve the dough and shape into two 13 cm/5 in diameter rounds. Place on a greased baking (cookie) sheet.

3 To make the topping, heat the oil in a pan and cook the onion for 2–3 minutes until softened. Add the mushrooms, garlic, tomatoes, nuts, parsley and ketchup and cook for 3–4 minutes, tossing well.

4 Pile the mixture in the centres of the potato rounds and top each with the Mascarpone cheese. Sprinkle with pepper.

5   Bake in a preheated oven at 190ºC/375ºF gas mark 5 for 15–20 minutes until the bases are golden brown. Serve with a mixed salad.

🕐 45 minutes

# Three-cheese Pasta with Pine Nuts

**Serves 2**

175g/6 oz penne or rigatoni pasta
15 g/½ oz/1 tbsp butter or margarine
50 g/2 oz/½ cup Parmesan cheese, grated
50 g/2 oz/½ cup Procaine cheese, grated
75 g/3 oz/¾ cup Mozzarella cheese, cubed
Salt and freshly ground black pepper
25 g/1 oz/¼ cup pine nuts, toasted
30 ml/2 tbsp chopped basil, chives or parsley
Green salad, to serve

1   Cook the pasta according to the packet directions. Drain and return to saucepan.

2   Stir in butter or margarine, all the cheeses and salt and pepper to taste. Toss well until combined and the cheeses have melted.

3   Add the pine nuts and herbs and toss again.

4   Serve immediately with a green salad.

🕐 20 minutes

✶   If you don't have any of these fresh herbs, just substitute pesto sauce, or use my nut-free pesto on page 13.

# Three-mushroom Platter

**Serves 2**

15 ml/1 tbsp olive oil
1 small red onion, peeled and thinly sliced
1 garlic clove, crushed
50 g/2 oz button mushrooms
50 g/2 oz chestnut mushrooms
50 g/2 oz oyster mushrooms
4 spring onions (scallions), thinly sliced
8 cherry tomatoes, halved
Grated rind and juice of ½ lime
Salt and freshly ground black pepper
15 ml/1 tbsp chopped parsley
French bread or pitta breads, to serve

1 Heat the oil in a frying pan (skillet) and fry (sauté) the onion for 2 minutes until softened.

2 Add the garlic and the button and chestnut mushrooms and cook for 2 minutes.

3 Add the oyster mushrooms, spring onions, tomatoes and lime rind. Toss well and cook for 2 minutes until the mushrooms have softened. Season to taste with salt and pepper.

4 Transfer to warm plates, sprinkle with the lime juice and parsley and serve with warm French breads or pitta breads.

🕐 20 minutes

✳ For a variation, substitute lemon rind and juice for lime.

# Sun-dried Tomato and Goats' Cheese Jackets

**Serves 2**

2 baking potatoes, about 200 g/7 oz each
Salt and freshly ground black pepper
6 sun-dried tomatoes in oil, drained and sliced
2.5 ml/½ tsp chopped garlic
15 ml/1 tbsp chopped basil
75 g/3 oz goats' cheese, thinly sliced
Crisp green salad, to serve

1 Prick the potatoes with a fork and rub with salt. Bake on the top shelf of a preheated oven at 200°C/400°F/gas mark 6 for 45–50 minutes until tender.

2 Place the tomatoes, garlic, basil and seasoning in a bowl and mix well.

3 Remove the potatoes from the oven and make three deep cuts lengthways in each.

4 Divide the goats' cheese and the tomato mixture between the cuts and return to the oven for a further 5–8 minutes until the cheese begins to melt.

5 Serve with a crisp green salad.

⏱ 1 hour

✱ For a variation, substitute Mozzarella for goats' cheese. You can reduce the cooking time by microwaving the potatoes on High for 10–20 minutes, then transferring them to the oven at step 4.

# Leek and Blue Cheese Lasagne

**Serves 2**

50 g/2 oz/¼ cup butter or margarine
450 g/1 lb small leeks, chopped
5 fresh pasta sheets
50 g/2 oz/½ cup Danish blue cheese, crumbled
Salt and freshly ground black pepper
150 ml/¼ pt/⅔ cup hot water
Mixed green salad leaves and cherry tomatoes, to serve

1   Heat the butter or margarine in a pan and fry (sauté) the leeks for 4–5 minutes until softened.

2   Grease a 15 x 10 cm/6 x 4 in baking dish. Cut the pasta sheets to make three equal portions and lay a third in the bottom of the dish.

3   Spread a third of the leeks over the pasta and sprinkle with a third of the cheese. Season with salt and pepper, then repeat with two more layers.

4   Pour the hot water around the edge of the dish and cover with foil. Bake in a preheated oven at 200°C/400°F/gas mark 6 for 30–40 minutes until the liquid has been absorbed.

5   Remove the foil and cook for a few more minutes until the top is golden brown. Serve with mixed green salad leaves and cherry tomatoes.

🕐 **50 minutes**

✳ Any crumbly cheese works well for this recipe.

# Vermicelli with Parmesan and Pesto

**Serves 2**
60 ml/4 tbsp olive oil
1 small onion, finely chopped
2.5 ml/½ tsp crushed garlic
25 g/1 oz/½ cup fresh wholemeal breadcrumbs
30 ml/2 tbsp chopped parsley
Salt and freshly ground black pepper
100 g/4 oz vermicelli
30 ml/2 tbsp pesto sauce
60 ml/4 tbsp grated Parmesan cheese
Spinach salad or green salad and crusty bread, to serve

1 Heat the oil in a pan and fry (sauté) the onion and garlic for 3–4 minutes to soften.

2 Add the breadcrumbs and parsley and cook for another 3 minutes. Season to taste.

3 Cook the vermicelli for about 2–3 minutes until al dente, then drain. Add the pesto and toss well.

4 Return to the heat, add the breadcrumb mixture and Parmesan and toss until mixed and heated through.

5 Serve with a spinach or green salad and crusty bread.

## ⏱ 20 minutes

✳ For a nut-free pesto, see page 13.

# Five-cheese Tortellini with Spinach Carbonara

### Serves 2

300 g/11 oz/1 packet of tortellini with five cheeses
100 g/4 oz ready-to-eat baby spinach
350 g/12 oz/1 medium jar of fresh carbonara sauce
Salt and freshly ground black pepper
25 g/1 oz/¼ cup Parmesan cheese, grated
25 g/1 oz/1 small packet of garlic and herb mini croûtons
Mixed green and tomato salad and French bread, to serve

1 Cook the tortellini according to the packet directions.

2 Meanwhile, place the spinach in a pan with the carbonara sauce and bring to the boil, stirring constantly. Cook for 2–3 minutes until the spinach has wilted and the sauce is heated through.

3 Drain the tortellini, add to the spinach mixture, season to taste and stir well.

4 Transfer to a heatproof dish and sprinkle with the Parmesan. Place under a hot grill (broiler) for 4–5 minutes until the top is golden brown.

5 Sprinkle with the croûtons and serve with a mixed green and tomato salad and French bread.

## 20 minutes

✴ Any creamy sauce, such as white wine and mushroom, will work as a substitution for the carbonara sauce.

# Meat Dishes

Contrary to common belief, grilling (broiling) or frying (sautéing) meats are not the only quick cooking methods. Several short cuts can be used to reduce the cooking time of a recipe. Obviously, the more expensive cuts take less time to cook, but with the inclusion of ready-prepared ingredients in these recipes the cooking time is reduced even further. Ethnic foods are now very popular and I have included some recipes that can be prepared and cooked with the minimum of fuss.

# Baked Beef and Stout Pudding

### Serves 2

225 g/8 oz braising steak
8 shallots, peeled
25 g/1 oz button mushrooms
2 small carrots, sliced
175 ml/6 fl oz/¾ cup stout
60 ml/4 tbsp water
15 ml/1 tbsp gravy powder or granules
15 ml/1 tbsp tomato purée (paste)
10 ml/2 tsp plain (all-purpose) flour
Salt and freshly ground black pepper
30 ml/2 tbsp chopped parsley
175 g/6 oz/1 packet of suet pudding mix
Green vegetables, to serve

1  Place all the ingredients except half the parsley and the suet pudding mix in an ovenproof dish and mix until combined.

2  Add the remaining parsley to the suet pudding mix and make up according to the packet directions. Roll out and place on top of the meat mixture.

3  Cover with foil and bake in a preheated oven at 160°C/325°F/gas mark 3 for 1½–1¾ hours until the meat is tender. Remove the foil for the last 15 minutes cooking time to brown the crust.

4  Serve with green vegetables.

### 2 hours

✶  This dish has a long cooking time but since you can ignore it while it is cooking, it is still very easy and worth the wait!

56

# Stir-fried Gingered Beef with Black Bean Sauce

### Serves 2

15 ml/1 tbsp vegetable oil
175 g/6 oz rump steak, thinly sliced
2.5 ml/½ tsp crushed garlic
15 ml/1 tbsp grated root ginger
30 ml/2 tbsp black bean sauce
2.5 ml/½ tsp sugar
50 g/2 oz shiitake mushrooms, thinly sliced
60 ml/4 tbsp water
4 spring onions (scallions), sliced
Salt and freshly ground black pepper
2 spring onions, shredded lengthways, to garnish
Boiled rice and Chinese vegetables, to serve

1  Heat the oil in a wok or frying pan (skillet), add the steak and cook for 2 minutes, tossing well, until lightly browned.

2  Add the garlic, ginger, black bean sauce and sugar and cook, stirring constantly, for 3 minutes.

3  Add the mushrooms, water and sliced spring onions and cook for 5 minutes.

4  Season to taste, garnish with the shredded onions and serve with boiled rice and Chinese vegetables.

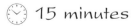 15 minutes

# Beef Satay Sticks

## Serves 2

225 g/8 oz rump steak, cut into thin strips
*For the marinade:*
15 ml/1 tbsp lime juice
15 ml/1 tbsp dark soy sauce
7.5 ml/1½ tsp chopped garlic
5 ml/1 tsp grated root ginger
10 ml/2 tsp olive oil
7.5 ml/1½ tsp chilli paste
*For the satay sauce:*
45 ml/3 tbsp smooth peanut butter
7.5 ml/1½ tsp chopped garlic
5 ml/1 tsp grated root ginger
10 ml/2 tsp oil
15 ml/1 tbsp light brown sugar
30 ml/2 tbsp water
Lime wedges, to garnish
Boiled egg noodles or fried (sautéed) rice, to serve

1  Thread the beef on to metal skewers in little pleats and place in a dish.

2  Mix together the marinade ingredients, brush over the meat and chill.

3  To make the satay sauce, place all the ingredients in a saucepan, heat gently and stir until blended.

4  Grill (broil) the beef skewers for 4–5 minutes, turning frequently, until browned and cooked through.

5  Lay the kebabs on plates, garnish with lime wedges and serve with the satay sauce and egg noodles or fried rice.

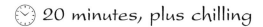 20 minutes, plus chilling

# Rosti-topped Bourgignon Bake

**Serves 2**

450 g/1 lb potatoes, washed but unpeeled
225 g/8 oz lean minced (ground) beef
50 g/2 oz chestnut mushrooms, quartered
225 g/8 oz/1 jar of Bourgignonne sauce
2.5 ml/½ tsp crushed garlic
1 onion, thinly sliced
25 g/1 oz/2 tbsp butter or margarine
Salt and freshly ground black pepper
Green vegetables, to serve

1   Cook the potatoes in salted water for 8 minutes. Drain and cover with a cloth to absorb the moisture.

2   Dry-fry the beef and mushrooms for 4–5 minutes until browned. Stir in the jar of sauce and bring to the boil, stirring well. Transfer to an ovenproof dish.

3   Fry (sauté) the garlic and onion in the butter or margarine for a few minutes until soft.

4   Peel and coarsely grate the potatoes into a bowl, add the onion and garlic and season to taste. Use two forks to toss the mixture.

5   Spoon the potato mixture over the mince, level the top and bake in a preheated oven at 220°C/425°F/gas mark 7 for 25–30 minutes until golden. Serve with green vegetables.

⏱ 50 minutes

✶   If you want a vegetarian version of this dish, you can use Quorn or soya mince. Use a potato such as Maris Piper for this recipe.

# Gruyère-stuffed Meatcakes

**Serves 2**

225 g/8 oz lean minced (ground) beef
1 small red onion, chopped
2.5 ml/½ tsp garlic purée (paste)
2.5 ml/½ tsp chopped parsley
Salt and freshly ground pepper
50 g/2 oz Gruyère (Swiss) cheese, cut into 4 pieces
Crisp salad and new potatoes, to serve

1 Place all the ingredients except the cheese in a bowl and mix to combine. Shape into four rounds.

2 Carefully make a cut into the centre of each and insert a piece of cheese. Reshape into a round, making sure the cheese is sealed inside the meatcake.

3 Grill (broil) or fry (sauté) for 8–10 minutes, turning occasionally during cooking.

4 Serve with a crisp salad and new potatoes.

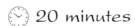 **20 minutes**

# Thatched Chilli Beef

**Serves 2**

225 g/8 oz braising steak, diced
1 small onion, roughly chopped
200 g/7 oz/½ large can of chopped tomatoes with garlic
150 ml/¼ pt/⅔ cup beef gravy
5 ml/1 tsp chilli paste
400 g/14 oz/1 large can of red kidney beans
1 small red (bell) pepper, roughly chopped
Salt and freshly ground black pepper
150 g/5 oz frozen prepared potato skins
25 g/1 oz/¼ cup Cheddar cheese, grated
Green vegetables or baby sweetcorn (corn), to serve

1  Place the steak, onion, tomatoes, gravy and chilli paste in a casserole dish (Dutch oven). Mix well, cover and cook in a preheated oven at 180°C/350°F/gas mark 4 for 1–1¼ hours until the meat is tender.

2  Stir in the kidney beans and red pepper and season to taste.

3  Scatter the potato skins on top and sprinkle with the cheese. Return to the oven and bake uncovered for a further 20 minutes until the potato skins are golden brown and crispy and the cheese has melted.

4  Serve with green vegetables or baby sweetcorn.

## ⏱ 2 hours

✶  Although this recipe has a long cooking time, it doesn't take long to prepare and once in the oven you can ignore it until it is ready to enjoy.

# Hash Cakes with Fried Eggs

**Serves 2**

30 ml/2 tbsp vegetable oil
1 small onion, chopped
225 g/8 oz potatoes, cooked and mashed
50 g/2 oz peas, cooked
200 g/7 oz/1 small can of corned beef, chilled overnight and
cut into 1 cm/½ in cubes
1 small egg, beaten
Salt and freshly ground black pepper
15 g/½ oz/1 tbsp butter or margarine
30 ml/2 tbsp pickle, brown sauce, tomato sauce or mustard
2 large eggs, fried (sautéed)

1  Heat half the oil and fry (sauté) the onion for 3–4 minutes
   until softened. Transfer to a large bowl.

2  Add the potato, peas, corned beef, beaten egg and
   seasoning to taste. Mix well and divide into two.

3  Shape into two 2 cm/¾ in thick cakes and chill for
   10 minutes.

4  Heat the remaining oil and the butter or margarine in a
   frying pan (skillet) and cook the cakes over a medium heat
   for a few minutes on each side until golden brown and
   heated through.

5  Serve topped with pickle, sauce or mustard and a fried egg.

### ⏱ 20 minutes, plus chilling

✣ Cabbage can be substituted for the peas, and bacon, ham
   or luncheon meat for the corned beef.

# Honey and Mustard Lamb with Minted Couscous

### Serves 2

225 g/8 oz lamb cutlets
30 ml/2 tbsp honey and mustard salad dressing
100 g/4 oz couscous
30 ml/2 tbsp chopped mint
8 cherry tomatoes, halved
25 g/1 oz/¼ cup flaked (slivered) almonds, toasted
Salt and freshly ground black pepper

1   Place the lamb in a shallow dish, pour the honey and mustard dressing over and leave to marinade for 30 minutes, turning once.

2   Prepare the couscous according to the packet directions and stir in the mint. Cover and leave to absorb the water.

3   Cook the lamb under a medium grill (broiler) for 6–7 minutes each side until cooked through and golden brown.

4   Fluff up the couscous with a fork and stir in the tomatoes and almonds. Season to taste with salt and pepper.

5   Spoon the couscous on to a serving dish, arrange the cutlets on top and drizzle any remaining dressing and juices over. Serve immediately.

### 🕐 20 minutes, plus marinating

✱   You can use thinly sliced (bell) pepper and chopped canned pineapple instead of the tomatoes for an equally delicious result.

# Kasbah Lamb with Apricots

### Serves 2

2.5 ml/½ tsp ground coriander (cilantro)
2.5 ml/½ tsp ground cumin
275 g/10 oz lamb, diced
15 ml/1 tbsp olive oil
2.5 ml/½ tsp garlic purée (paste)
2.5 ml/½ tsp chilli paste
1 small onion, sliced
200 g/7 oz/½ large can of chopped tomatoes
75 g/3 oz/½ cup dried apricots, halved
10 ml/2 tsp chopped coriander
10 ml/2 tsp chopped parsley
Salt and freshly ground black pepper
Marrakesh Couscous (page 100), to serve

1  Place the ground coriander and cumin in a bowl, add the lamb and toss well to coat.

2  Heat the oil, add the garlic purée, chilli paste and onion and cook for 2 minutes until softened. Add the lamb and toss for 2–3 minutes until browned.

3  Add the tomatoes and apricots, cover, reduce the heat and simmer for 45 minutes.

4  Add the chopped coriander and parsley and season to taste. Cover and simmer for 20 minutes.

5  Serve with Marrakesh Couscous.

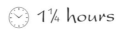 1¼ hours

# Minted Lamb Koftas

**Serves 2**

225 g/8 oz minced (ground) lamb
2.5 ml/½ tsp crushed garlic
15 ml/1 tbsp chopped fresh mint
30 ml/2 tbsp fresh white breadcrumbs
Salt and freshly ground black pepper
15 ml/1 tbsp olive oil
½ x 350 g/½ x 12 oz/½ medium jar of fruity hot jalfrezi sauce
Boiled rice and naan breads, to serve

1  Place the lamb, garlic, mint, breadcrumbs and seasoning in a bowl. Mix to combine, then shape into eight meatballs.

2  Heat the oil in a frying pan (skillet) and fry (sauté) the meatballs over a low heat for 8–10 minutes, turning frequently, until browned on all sides.

3  Remove the meatballs from pan, skim off the oil from the juices and add the jalfrezi sauce. Return the meatballs to the pan, cover and simmer for 5 minutes until heated through and the sauce is hot.

4  Serve with boiled rice and naan breads.

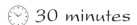 30 minutes

# Lamb and Spinach Balti

### Serves 2
10 ml/2 tsp vegetable oil
225 g/8 oz lamb leg steaks, cut into thin strips
5 ml/1 tsp chopped garlic
5 ml/1 tsp chopped root ginger
10 ml/2 tsp garam masala
100 g/4 oz tomatoes, cut into wedges
50 g/2 oz mushrooms, quartered
50 g/2 oz baby leaf spinach
Boiled rice and naan breads, to serve

1 Heat the oil in a wok or frying pan (skillet), add the meat and toss for 4–5 minutes until sealed and turning brown.

2 Add the garlic, ginger and garam masala and cook for 2 minutes.

3 Add the tomatoes and mushrooms and cook for 5 minutes, tossing well.

4 Add the spinach and cook for a further 2 minutes, tossing well to combine the ingredients.

5 Serve with boiled rice and naan breads.

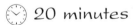 20 minutes

# Spicy Lamb Filo Parcels

**Serves 2**

225 g/8 oz minced (ground) lamb
1 small onion, peeled and finely chopped
5 ml/1 tsp chopped mint
2.5 ml/½ tsp ground cumin
2.5 ml/½ tsp curry powder or paste
15 ml/1 tbsp sun-dried tomato purée (paste)
Salt and freshly ground black pepper
4 filo pastry (paste) sheets, halved
1 small egg white, beaten
Ratatouille, to serve

1  Place the lamb, onion, mint, cumin and curry powder or paste in a saucepan, cover with a lid and dry-fry for 5–7 minutes, stirring occasionally.

2  Stir in the tomato purée and cook, uncovered, for 5 minutes. Season with salt and pepper.

3  Lay one sheet of filo pastry on a baking tray, brush with egg white and lay another sheet on top. Repeat with two more sheets of pastry. Spoon half the lamb mixture into the middle, gather up the pastry and pinch together at the top to form a parcel. Repeat with the other pastry sheets.

4  Brush with egg white, then bake in a preheated oven at 200°C/400°F/gas mark 6 for 10 minutes until browned.

5  Serve with ratatouille.

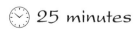 25 minutes

# Oriental Lamb Stir-fry

**Serves 2**

15 ml/1 tbsp oil for stir-frying
225 g/8 oz lamb leg steaks, cut into thin strips
100 g/4 oz mangetout (snow peas)
2 small carrots, peeled and cut into matchsticks
6 spring onions (scallions), diagonally sliced
150 g/5 oz/1 small jar of ginger and honey stir-fry sauce
50 g/2 oz water chestnuts, sliced
Egg noodles, to serve

1 Heat the oil in a wok or frying pan (skillet) and fry (sauté) the lamb for 5 minutes, tossing well, until lightly browned.

2 Add the mangetout, carrots and spring onions. Toss for a further 2–3 minutes.

3 Add the stir-fry sauce and water chestnuts. Toss continuously for a further 3–4 minutes until all the ingredients are cooked and heated through.

4 Serve on a bed of egg noodles.

🕐 20 minutes

✶ For a variation, substitute chicken, pork or beef for the lamb and sweetcorn (corn) or broccoli for the mangetout.

# Creamy Pan-fried Pork with Shiitake Mushrooms

### Serves 2

10 ml/2 tsp olive oil
225 g/8 oz pork fillet, cut into 6 slices
75 g/3 oz shiitake or oyster mushrooms, roughly sliced
150 ml/¼ pt/⅔ cup white wine
100 ml/3½ fl oz/scant ½ cup crème fraîche
5 ml/1 tsp wholegrain mustard
Salt and freshly ground black pepper
New potatoes, or basmati rice seasoned with finely grated
lemon rind, and French (green) beans, to serve

1 Heat the oil in a frying pan (skillet) and fry (sauté) the pork for 5–6 minutes, turning frequently, until lightly browned and cooked. Remove from the pan and keep warm.

2 Add the mushrooms to the pan, toss well and cook for 2 minutes. Remove and keep warm with the pork.

3 Add the wine, stir and cook rapidly for 3–4 minutes until the liquid has thickened and reduced by half.

4 Reduce the heat and stir in the crème fraîche and mustard. Return the pork and mushrooms to the pan, season to taste and simmer gently for a further 4–5 minutes, coating the pork with the sauce during cooking.

5 Serve with new potatoes or basmati rice and beans.

### 🕐 30 minutes

✶ If oyster or shiitake mushroom are not available, use chestnut or button mushrooms instead.

# Pan-fried Pork with Redcurrant Sauce

**Serves 2**
10 ml/2 tsp olive oil
6 thin-cut pork steaks
150 ml/¼ pt/⅔ cup chicken stock
Grated rind and juice of ½ orange
15 ml/1 tbsp sherry
10 ml/2 tsp redcurrant jelly (clear conserve)
5 ml/1 tsp chopped sage
Salt and freshly ground black pepper
Shredded cabbage and creamed potatoes, to serve

1 Heat the oil in a frying pan (skillet) and fry (sauté) the steaks for 3–4 minutes on each side until cooked. Remove from the pan and keep warm.

2 Add the stock, orange rind and juice, sherry and redcurrant jelly to the pan and stir to combine. Boil for 2–3 minutes until reduced slightly and darkened in colour.

3 Stir in the sage, season to taste and return the steaks to the pan.

4 Cook until heated through, then arrange on a bed of freshly cooked shredded cabbage and serve with creamed potatoes.

⏱ 20 minutes

# Country Orchard Pork Steaks

**Serves 2**

1 red eating (dessert) apple, cored and thickly sliced
75 ml/5 tbsp water
25 g/1 oz/2 tbsp butter or margarine
2 pork steaks, about 100 g/4 oz each
4 spring onions (scallions), finely chopped
150 ml/¼ pt/⅔ cup dry cider
30 ml/2 tbsp crème fraîche
Salt and freshly ground black pepper
New potatoes tossed in herb butter and mangetout
(snow peas), to serve

1   Place the apple in a pan with the water, bring to the boil, cover and simmer for 2–3 minutes until just tender. Drain.

2   Heat half the butter or margarine and fry (sauté) the steaks for 5 minutes on each side. Remove and keep warm.

3   Add the remaining butter or margarine to the pan and fry the spring onions for 2 minutes. Pour in the cider, bring to the boil and cook for about 5 minutes until the sauce is reduced by half.

4   Stir in the crème fraîche, return the steaks to pan and coat with the sauce. Add the apples, season and heat through.

5   Serve with new potatoes in herb butter and mangetout.

✣ 25 minutes

✱ The cider may be replaced with apple juice if you prefer. Add a squeeze of lemon juice at step 4 if you like a sharper-flavoured sauce.

# Stuffed Pork Escalopes

**Serves 2**

2 pork escalopes, about 100 g/4 oz each
10 ml/2 tsp sun-dried tomato purée (paste)
10 ml/2 tsp chopped parsley
75 g/3 oz apricot and pecan stuffing mix, made up and cooled
10 ml/2 tsp olive oil
New potatoes tossed in wholegrain mustard and roasted
vegetables, to serve

1   Lay the escalopes between two pieces of clingfilm (plastic wrap) and beat with a rolling pin to flatten them. Spread the tomato purée on to each and sprinkle with the parsley.

2   Spoon the stuffing in the centre of each escalope, fold up to make two parcels and tie with string. Place on a baking tray.

3   Brush with the oil and bake in a preheated oven at 180°C/350°F/gas mark 4 for 25–30 minutes until browned and cooked through.

4   Remove the string and slice the parcels into rings.

5   Serve with new potatoes tossed in wholegrain mustard and roasted vegetables.

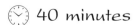 40 minutes

# Tandoori Pork Bites with Mango Yoghurt

**Serves 2**

200 g/7 oz minced (ground) pork
25 g/1 oz/½ cup fresh white breadcrumbs
1 small onion, finely chopped
5 ml/1 tsp lemon juice
5–10 ml/1–2 tsp tandoori paste
10 ml/2 tsp vegetable oil
45 ml/3 tbsp mango chutney
15 ml/1 tbsp plain yoghurt
Pilau rice, to serve

1   Place the pork, breadcrumbs, onion and lemon juice in a bowl. Add the tandoori paste to taste and mix well to combine. Shape into 16 balls.

2   Heat the oil in a frying pan (skillet) and fry (sauté) the pork bites for 7–8 minutes, tossing well to brown on all sides. Drain on kitchen paper (paper towels).

3   Mix the mango chutney with the yoghurt and serve with the pork bites and pilau rice.

⊙ **25 minutes**

✶   For a variation, substitute minced chicken or lamb for the pork.

# Gammon Steaks with Port and Plum Glaze

**Serves 2**

2 gammon steaks, about 175 g/6 oz each
*For the port and plum glaze:*
45 ml/3 tbsp plum jam (jelly)
15 ml/1 tbsp apple juice
15 ml/1 tbsp port
A pinch of ground cloves
2.5 ml/½ tsp arrowroot
5 ml/1 tsp water
New potatoes and runner beans, to serve

1   Snip the rind of the gammon to prevent the steaks curling.

2   Grill (broil) or fry (sauté) on a medium heat for 4 minutes on each side until cooked through.

3   To make the glaze, place the jam, apple juice, port and cloves in a saucepan and bring to the boil.

4   Blend the arrowroot with the water, then stir it into the sauce and simmer gently, stirring continuously, until thickened.

5   Pour the glaze over the steaks and serve with new potatoes and runner beans.

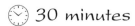 30 minutes

# Chorizo and Courgette Pilau

**Serves 2**

25 g/1 oz/2 tbsp butter or margarine
1 onion, chopped
2.5 ml/½ tsp chopped garlic
100 g/4 oz chorizo sausage, diced
225 g/8 oz/1 cup basmati rice
600 ml/1 pt/2½ cups chicken stock
2 small courgettes (zucchini), diced
Salt and freshly ground black pepper
Chopped parsley and lemon wedges, to garnish
Crusty bread and a green salad, to serve

1 Heat the butter or margarine in a flameproof casserole dish (Dutch oven) and fry (sauté) the onion and garlic for 3–4 minutes until softened.

2 Add the chorizo and cook for a further 3 minutes.

3 Add the rice and toss well to coat.

4 Add the stock and courgette and season to taste with salt and pepper. Bring to the boil, stir and cover with a tight-fitting lid.

5 Cook in a preheated oven at 180°C/350°F/gas mark 4 for 15 minutes until the rice is tender. Stir well, then garnish with parsley and lemon wedges and serve with crusty bread and a green salad.

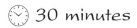 30 minutes

# Pancetta Tagliatelle in Creamy Sauce

**Serves 2**

175 g/6 oz tagliatelle
5 ml/1 tsp olive oil
4 slices of pancetta, cut into pieces
4 spring onions (scallions), chopped
15 ml/1 tbsp pumpkin seeds
60 ml/4 tbsp garlic and herb cream cheese
30 ml/2 tbsp milk
Freshly ground black pepper

1 Bring a large pan of salted water to the boil, add the tagliatelle and simmer, uncovered, for about 5 minutes until just tender.

2 Meanwhile, heat the oil in a saucepan and fry (sauté) the pancetta and spring onions for 2 minutes until soft. Remove them from the saucepan.

3 Toast the pumpkin seeds in a dry saucepan until golden, then remove.

4 Reduce the heat and add the cheese and milk to the saucepan, stirring well to make a smooth sauce.

5 Drain the pasta, then return it to the hot pan.

6 Stir in the cheese sauce, pumpkin seeds, pancetta and onions. Season to taste with pepper and serve immediately.

🕐 15 minutes

✴ Pancetta is an Italian dry-cured bacon. If you cannot find it, used ordinary bacon instead.

# Parma Romana

**Serves 2**

400 g/14 oz/1 large can of chopped tomatoes
5 ml/1 tsp chopped garlic
5 ml/1 tsp chilli paste
2.5 ml/1/2 tsp soft brown sugar
15 ml/1 tbsp chopped basil
Salt and freshly ground black pepper
200 g/7 oz pasta shapes
25 g/1 oz/¼ cup Parmesan cheese, grated
50 g/2 oz Parma ham, cut into thin slivers
Parmesan cheese shavings and whole basil leaves, to garnish
Italian bread, to serve

1  Place the tomatoes, garlic, chilli paste and sugar in a saucepan. Bring to the boil and simmer, uncovered, for 15 minutes until slightly reduced and thickened.

2  Add the chopped basil and season with salt and pepper. If a smooth sauce is required, sieve (strain) or blend in a food processor.

3  Meanwhile, bring a large saucepan of salted water to the boil, add the pasta and simmer, uncovered, for about 8–10 minutes until just tender.

4  Drain, then return to the saucepan and add the Parmesan cheese and tomato sauce. Heat through, tossing well to coat the pasta.

5  Add the Parma ham and toss again.

6  Garnish with Parmesan shavings and basil leaves and serve immediately with an Italian bread.

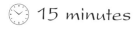 15 minutes

# Pesto and Mascarpone Carbonara

**Serves 2**

150 g/5 oz spaghetti
15 ml/1 tbsp green pesto sauce
50 g/2 oz/¼ cup Mascarpone cheese
50 g/2 oz Parma ham, sliced
15 ml/1 tbsp roughly torn basil leaves
Freshly ground black pepper
Sun-dried tomato bread, to serve

1  Cook the spaghetti according to the packet directions. Drain well and return to pan. Add the pesto and heat through gently.

2  Toss well to coat, then stir in the Mascarpone cheese and Parma ham. Add the basil and season with pepper.

3  Serve immediately with sun-dried tomato bread.

## 🕐 20 minutes

✳ For a vegetarian version of this recipe, substitute vegetarian rashers (slices) for the Parma ham or just omit the ham and add a little salt when seasoning.

✳ Always keep a jar of pesto in the fridge; you can toss it with hot pasta or spoon a little into plain yoghurt or fromage frais for a dip or pizza base. For a nut-free pesto, see page 13.

# Stuffed Portabella Mushrooms

**Serves 2**

4 portabella mushrooms
15 ml/1 tbsp olive oil
5 ml/1 tsp chopped garlic
1 small red or yellow (bell) pepper, diced
1 small red onion, chopped
15 ml/1 tbsp chopped parsley
2 back bacon rashers (slices), cooked and diced
45 ml/3 tbsp fresh white breadcrumbs, toasted
Salt and freshly ground black pepper
Mixed salad leaves, a soured (dairy sour) cream and chive dip
and crusty bread, to serve

1  Leaving the mushroom caps whole, remove and chop the stalks. Brush the caps with some of the oil and grill (broil), rounded-side up, for 3–4 minutes without turning.

2  Cook the garlic, diced pepper, mushroom stalks, onion and parsley in the remaining oil in a frying pan (skillet) for 2–3 minutes until softened. Add the bacon and breadcrumbs and season with salt and pepper.

3  Turn the mushroom caps over and fill the cavity with the stuffing. Grill for 4–5 minutes until tender and juicy.

4  Serve with mixed salad leaves, a soured cream and chive dip and crusty bread.

🕐 20 minutes

✷  You can use any large mushrooms for this recipe. To make a vegetarian dish, simply substitute vegetarian rashers for the bacon. This recipe also makes a tasty starter for four.

# Poultry Dishes

Poultry is so versatile and excellent value for money. It can be bought in the supermarket ready-prepared in a number of ways, which reduces the preparation time in a recipe. With the clever addition of seasonings, poultry need never lack flavour and a main meal or snack can be prepared very quickly.

# Pan-fried Chilli Chicken

**Serves 2**
1 lime, halved lengthways
1 onion, thickly sliced and separated into rings
30 ml/1 tbsp milk
15 ml/1 tbsp plain (all-purpose) flour
Salt and freshly ground black pepper
30 ml/2 tbsp olive oil
2 chicken portions, about 150 g/6 oz each
15 ml/1 tbsp chilli paste
5 ml/1 tsp grated fresh root ginger
1 fresh chilli, seeded and thinly sliced
A few parsley sprigs
Rocket or baby spinach leaves and savoury rice, to serve

1  Grate the rind and squeeze the juice from one lime half. Cut the other half into wedges and reserve for garnish.

2  Dip the onion rings in the milk, then toss in the flour seasoned with salt and pepper. Heat half the oil in a frying pan (skillet) and fry (sauté) the onions for about 2 minutes until golden brown. Remove from the pan and keep warm.

3  Heat the remaining oil in the pan, add the chicken and fry for 2–3 minutes on each side until golden brown. Remove from the pan.

4  Add the chilli paste, ginger and lime rind and juice to the pan and stir over a low heat to form a thick sauce. Return the chicken to the pan, cover and cook for about 20 minutes, turning occasionally, until cooked through.

5  Garnish the chicken and juices with the lime wedges, chilli and parsley sprigs. Serve with fresh rocket or baby spinach leaves and savoury rice.

# Chicken Milano

**Serves 2**
15 ml/1 tbsp olive oil
2 boneless chicken breasts, skinned and cut into thin strips
200 g/7 oz/1 small jar of pepper and tomato sauce
2.5 ml/½ tsp garlic purée (paste)
2.5 ml/½ tsp chilli paste
45 ml/3 tbsp chopped parsley
45 ml/3 tbsp crème fraîche
175 g/6 oz spaghetti

1 Heat the oil in a frying pan (skillet) and fry (sauté) the chicken until browned and cooked through. Remove from pan and keep warm.

2 Add the pepper and tomato sauce, garlic purée, chilli paste, 30 ml/2 tbsp of the parsley and the crème fraîche

3 Cook the spaghetti according to the packet directions, drain well and return to pan.

4 Add the chicken, pour the sauce over and heat through.

5 Serve sprinkled with the remaining parsley.

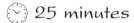 25 minutes

# Mediterranean Chicken

**Serves 2**

15 ml/1 tbsp olive oil
2 boneless chicken breasts, skinned
and cut into 1 cm/½ in slices
1 small aubergine (eggplant), thinly sliced
1 small courgette (zucchini), sliced
1 small yellow (bell) pepper, seeded and sliced
225 g/8 oz/1 medium jar of sun-ripened tomato
and basil sauce
225 g/8 oz penne pasta

1  Heat the oil in a pan and fry (sauté) the chicken breasts for 2–3 minutes, tossing well. Remove from the pan and keep warm.

2  Add the aubergine, courgette and pepper to the pan. Cook for 2–3 minutes, tossing well.

3  Return the chicken to the pan and pour the tomato and basil sauce over. Cover and simmer for 20 minutes, stirring occasionally.

4  Meanwhile, cook the pasta according to the packet directions, drain and return to the pan.

5  Add the chicken and sauce to the pan and heat through. Serve immediately on warm plates.

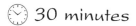 30 minutes

# Olive-stuffed Chicken Spirals

**Serves 2**

2 boneless chicken breasts, skinned
*For the olive filling:*
8 black olives, stoned (pitted)
8 green olives, stoned or stuffed with pimiento
30 ml/2 tbsp capers in vinegar
15 ml/1 tbsp sun-dried tomato purée (paste)
15 ml/1 tbsp chopped anchovy fillets or
5 ml/1 tsp anchovy paste
Rocket leaves, buttered new potatoes and
glazed carrots, to serve

1   Lay the chicken breasts between two pieces of clingfilm (plastic wrap) and beat with a rolling pin until doubled in size.

2   To make the olive filling, finely chop the olives and capers and mix thoroughly with the remaining ingredients.

3   Spread the filling over the chicken breasts, roll up and secure with cocktail sticks (toothpicks).

4   Bake in a preheated oven at 180°C/350°F/gas mark 4 for 20–25 minutes.

5   Remove the cocktail sticks, slice the breasts and serve on a bed of rocket leaves with buttered new potatoes and glazed carrots.

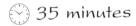 35 minutes

# Parmesan Crumb Chicken

### Serves 2

25 g/1 oz/½ cup fresh white breadcrumbs
15 ml/1 tbsp grated Parmesan cheese
2 boneless chicken breasts, skinned
15 ml/1 tbsp seasoned plain (all-purpose) flour
1 small egg, beaten
30 ml/2 tbsp olive oil
Lemon wedges, to garnish
Lollo rosso leaves and tomato wedges, to serve

1   Mix together the breadcrumbs and Parmesan.

2   Coat the chicken breasts in the flour, then dip into the egg, then dip in the breadcrumb mixture.

3   Heat the oil and cook the chicken for 8–10 minutes on each side until the coating is crisp and golden and the chicken is cooked through.

4   Garnish with lemon wedges and serve with crisp lollo rosso leaves and tomato wedges.

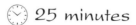 25 minutes

# Chicken Fajitas

**Serves 2**

2 chicken breasts, about 175 g/6 oz each, boned, skinned and thinly sliced

1 red or green (bell) pepper, seeded and thinly sliced

1 small onion, thinly sliced

15 ml/1 tbsp lime juice

15 ml/1 tbsp olive oil

5 ml/1 tsp paprika

5 ml/1 tsp chopped or puréed mild fresh chilli

5 ml/1 tsp chopped oregano

Salt and freshly ground black pepper

4 large flour tortillas

Soured (dairy sour) cream and a green salad, to serve

1  Place all the ingredients except the tortillas in a bowl. Mix well until combined.

2  Heat a wok or frying pan (skillet) and stir-fry the mixture over a high heat for about 5–7 minutes, tossing constantly, until browned and cooked through.

3  Warm the tortillas according to the packet directions and spoon the mixture into the centres.

4  Roll up and serve immediately with soured cream and a crisp green salad.

⏲ 20 minutes

✶  If you do not have any tortillas, spoon the mixture into split pitta breads.

# Turkey Stir-fry with Mango and Sesame

**Serves 2**

15 ml/1 tbsp sesame or other oil for stir-frying
175 g/6 oz stir-fry turkey pieces or turkey breast cut into thin strips
175 g/6 oz frozen stir-fry vegetables
*For the stir-fry sauce:*
7.5 ml/1½ tsp curry paste or powder
7.5 ml/1½ tsp made mustard
5 ml/1 tsp Worcestershire sauce
5 ml/1 tsp soy sauce
10 ml/2 tsp mango chutney
Tabasco sauce (optional)
2 spring onions (scallions), thinly sliced, and
15 ml/1 tbsp sesame seeds, to garnish
Beansprouts or egg noodles, to serve

1 Heat the oil in a wok or frying pan (skillet) and stir-fry the turkey on a high heat for 4–5 minutes. Remove with a slotted spoon and keep warm.

2 Add the stir-fry vegetables to the pan and cook according to the packet directions.

3 Mix together all the sauce ingredients in a bowl.

4 Return the turkey to the pan, pour the sauce over and toss until well mixed and heated through, adding a little water if necessary.

5 Sprinkle with the spring onions and sesame seeds and serve with beansprouts or egg noodles.

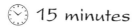 15 minutes

# Chicken and Ham en Croûte

**Serves 2**

350 g/12 oz puff pastry (paste), thawed if frozen
175 g/6 oz/1½ cups cooked chicken, diced
50 g/2 oz/½ cup cooked ham, diced
50 g/2 oz button mushrooms, halved
50 g/2 oz sweetcorn (corn)
250 g/9 oz/1 medium jar of white wine
and garlic cooking sauce
Salt and freshly ground black pepper
1 small egg, beaten
10 ml/2 tsp sesame seeds
Mixed salad leaves, to serve

1 Roll out the pastry to 5 mm/¼ in thick and cut into four 20 x 15 cm/8 x 6 in ovals.

2 Mix together the chicken, ham, mushrooms, sweetcorn, sauce and seasoning in a bowl.

3 Place two of the pastry ovals on a greased baking tray and spoon the chicken mixture on the centre of each to within 2 cm/¾ in of the edges.

4 Brush the edges with egg, place a pastry lid on top and seal the edges together with finger and thumb. Glaze with egg and make a small slit in the top of each. Sprinkle with the sesame seeds.

5 Bake in a preheated oven at 190°C/375°F/gas mark 5 for 20–25 minutes until risen and golden brown.

6   Serve with mixed salad leaves.

### ⏱ 40 minutes

✳   For a variation, you can substitute the same quantity of cooked turkey for the chicken.

# Chicken Pitta Pockets

**Serves 2**

15 ml/1 tbsp tomato purée (paste)
15 ml/1 tbsp clear honey
10 ml/2 tsp Worcestershire sauce
5 ml/1 tsp soy sauce
2 small boneless chicken breasts, skinned and cut into strips
2 large pitta breads
Crisp lettuce leaves
2 sun-blush tomatoes, sliced

1   Mix together the tomato purée, honey, Worcestershire sauce and soy sauce. Add the chicken strips and toss well.

2   Remove the chicken from the marinade and grill (broil) or fry (sauté) for 8–10 minutes on a moderate heat, turning gently to prevent sticking. Bring the marinade to the boil in a small saucepan and simmer for 2 minutes (or microwave on High for 1 minute, stirring halfway through cooking).

3   Open out each pitta bread to form a pocket and divide the salad leaves and tomato slices between them. Top with the chicken strips and spoon some of the marinade over.

### ⏱ 15 minutes

# Coronation Chicken Tortillas

**Serves 2**

2 flour tortillas
5 ml/1 tsp curry paste
60 ml/4 tbsp mayonnaise
15 ml/1 tbsp smooth apricot jam (jelly)
5 ml/1 tsp chopped parsley
A squeeze of lemon juice
Salt and freshly ground black pepper
175 g/6 oz chicken breast, cooked, skinned and sliced into thin strips
1 celery stick, thinly sliced
½ red eating (dessert) apple, thinly sliced
4 iceberg lettuce leaves, shredded

1 Prepare the tortillas according to the packet directions.

2 Soften the curry paste over a pan of warm water, then allow to cool. Add the mayonnaise, jam, parsley, lemon juice and salt and pepper to taste and mix well.

3 Stir in the chicken, celery and apple.

4 Arrange the lettuce on the tortillas and top with the chicken mixture. Roll up and serve immediately.

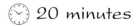 20 minutes

# Turkey Satay Sticks

**Serves 2**

225 g/8 oz turkey steaks
30 ml/2 tbsp clear honey
15 ml/1 tbsp smooth or crunchy peanut butter
15 ml/1 tbsp lemon juice
30 ml/2 tbsp chopped parsley
1 red onion, peeled and cut into chunks
30 ml/2 tbsp olive oil
4 spring onions (scallions), trimmed
Beansprouts or egg noodles, to serve

1 Cut the turkey into long 5 mm/¼ in thick and 5 cm/2 in wide strips. Place in a non-metallic bowl.

2 Mix together the honey, peanut butter, lemon juice and parsley and spoon over the turkey, tossing to coat thoroughly. Cover and chill for at least 2 hours, turning once or twice.

3 Thread the turkey and red onion chunks alternately on to soaked wooden skewers. Brush the onion chunks with some of the oil.

4 Cook on a barbecue or under a hot grill (broiler) for about 10 minutes until tender and cooked through, basting occasionally with any remaining marinade.

5 Meanwhile, brush the spring onions with the remaining oil and gently cook with the kebabs for the last 3 minutes of cooking time.

6 Serve with beansprouts or egg noodles.

🕐 20 minutes, plus marinating

✳ For a more intense flavour, marinate the turkey overnight. This will also tenderise the meat.

# Turkey Steaks with Oyster Mushrooms

**Serves 2**

50 g/2 oz streaky bacon, chopped
15 g/½ oz/1 tbsp butter or margarine
2 turkey steaks, about 100 g/4 oz each
15 ml/1 tbsp plain (all-purpose) flour
250 ml/8 fl oz/1 cup dry white wine
100 g/4 oz oyster mushrooms, sliced
1.5 ml/¼ tsp garlic purée (paste)
45 ml/3 tbsp crème fraîche
5 ml/1 tsp rosemary leaves
Salt and freshly ground pepper
Mashed potato and broccoli or asparagus spears, to serve

1 Dry-fry the bacon for 1 minute, then remove from the pan.

2 Add the butter or margarine to the pan and fry (sauté) the turkey steaks for 5 minutes, turning once. Remove from the pan.

3 Add the flour to the pan and cook for 1 minute. Stir in the wine and bring to boil.

4 Add the mushrooms, garlic purée, crème fraîche and rosemary to the pan and season to taste.

5 Return the turkey steaks and bacon to the pan and coat with the sauce. Cover and simmer for 25 minutes, basting occasionally with the sauce, until the steaks are tender.

6 Serve with creamy mashed potato and broccoli or asparagus spears.

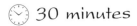 30 minutes

# Vegetables, Snacks and Dips

An exciting vegetable accompaniment can enhance any plainly cooked meat or fish dish. Many of the side dishes included in this book would make a delicious light lunch or supper dish served with a crisp salad. The use of garnishes will also brighten up the dullest of cooked vegetables and snacks.

A traditional sandwich can be boring, so I have included some imaginative quick and easy to prepare snacks to satisfy your hunger pangs.

A dip adds an exciting flavour to any plainly cooked meat, fish or vegetable dish. They are also a good accompaniment to brighten up barbecued foods, salads and cold meats.

# Charred Corn Cobs with Fiery Glaze

**Serves 2**

2 corn on the cob, husks removed
*For the glaze:*
15 ml/1 tbsp olive oil
15 g/½ oz/1 tbsp butter or margarine, melted
5 ml/1 tsp grated lime rind
2.5 ml/½ tsp chilli paste
15 ml/1 tbsp chopped coriander (cilantro)
Garlic salt
Freshly ground black pepper

1 Cut two pieces of foil large enough to wrap each corn cob. Place the corn in the centre.

2 Mix together the glaze ingredients in a bowl.

3 Brush the corn with the glaze, then fold the foil to form a parcel.

4 Cook under a moderate grill (broiler) for 10–15 minutes, turning occasionally, until the kernels are tender.

5 Unwrap the parcels and serve with any remaining glaze basted over the cobs.

🕐 20 minutes

✳ The cobs are delicious served on their own and also make an ideal accompaniment to grilled (broiled) or barbecued meats.

# Honey and Mustard Roasted Vegetables

**Serves 2**

2 potatoes, peeled and cut into wedges
2 carrots, peeled and cut into wedges
2 parsnips, peeled and cut into wedges
8 shallots, peeled
*For the glaze:*
30 ml/2 tbsp olive oil
30 ml/2 tbsp wholegrain mustard
30 ml/2 tbsp honey
Salt and freshly ground black pepper

1   Blanch the vegetables in hot water for 5 minutes. Drain and place in a roasting tin (pan).

2   Mix together the glaze ingredients and pour over the vegetables. Toss well to coat.

3   Cook in a preheated oven at 200°C/400°F/gas mark 6 for 20–25 minutes, tossing once during cooking.

### 35 minutes

✳ These vegetables go very well with roasted and grilled (broiled) meats.

# Indian Spiced Potato Wraps

### Serves 2

10 ml/2 tsp lime pickle
5 ml/1 tsp sun-dried tomato purée (paste)
2.5 ml/½ tsp curry powder
15 ml/1 tbsp plain yoghurt
7.5 ml/1½ tsp olive oil
250 g/9 oz baby new potatoes, cooked
75 g/3 oz streaky bacon

1   Mix together the pickle, tomato purée, curry powder, yoghurt and oil in a bowl. Add the potatoes and toss well to coat.

2   Wrap a piece of bacon round each potato.

3   Grill (broil) or barbecue for 10–15 minutes, turning frequently and basting with any remaining marinade.

### 🕐 20 minutes

✷   Serve these potatoes with grilled (broiled) or barbecued meats. Vegetarians can simply omit the bacon wrapping.

# Potato Wedges with Paprika and Feta Cheese

### Serves 2

2 large potatoes, each cut into 8 wedges
15 ml/1 tbsp olive oil
10 ml/2 tsp paprika
Freshly ground black pepper
50 g/2 oz/½ cup Feta cheese, crumbled

1  Place the potatoes in a pan of salted water and boil until just cooked but not broken. Drain and return to the pan.

2  Add the oil, paprika and pepper to the potatoes and toss well, taking care not to break them.

3  Transfer to a roasting tin (pan) or heatproof dish, sprinkle with the cheese and place under a hot grill (broiler) for 2–3 minutes until the cheese is golden and bubbling.

### 10 minutes

✶  You can serve this dish as a starter or snack on its own, and also as an accompaniment to cold meat and salad.

# Roasted Garlic with Potatoes

**Serves 2**

2 small garlic bulbs
30 ml/2 tbsp olive oil
350 g/12 oz baking potatoes, peeled and cut into large chunks
Salt and freshly ground black pepper
Chopped parsley, to garnish

1   Separate the garlic bulbs into cloves but leave them unpeeled.

2   Place the oil in an ovenproof dish and heat in a preheated oven at 200°C/400°F/gas mark 6 for 4–5 minutes.

3   Add the garlic and potato and toss well to coat with the oil. Bake for 30–45 minutes, tossing half-way through the cooking time, until golden brown.

4   Season with salt and pepper and garnish with the parsley before serving. The garlic will easily pop out of its skin while cooking or eating.

🕐 1 hour

✶   Serve this with roasted and grilled (broiled) meats or, for a supper dish, add 100 g/4 oz/1 cup diced cooked ham or gammon pieces and some sliced mushrooms 10 minutes before the end of the cooking time.

# Roasted Spiced Root Vegetables

**Serves 2**

30 ml/2 tbsp olive oil
2 small parsnips, cut into bite-sized chunks
2 carrots, cut into bite-sized chunks
½ small swede (rutabaga), cut into bite-sized chunks
½ small acorn squash, cut into bite-sized chunks
5 ml/1 tsp mustard seeds, coarsely crushed
5 ml/1 tsp coriander (cilantro) seeds, coarsely crushed
2.5 ml/½ tsp cumin seeds, coarsely crushed
15 ml/1 tbsp clear honey
Salt and freshly ground black pepper

1  Heat the oil in a roasting tin (pan), add the vegetables and toss well to coat. Fry (sauté), stirring occasionally, until lightly browned.

2  Add the spices, honey and seasoning and toss.

3  Roast in a preheated oven at 220°C/425°F/gas mark 7 for 25–30 minutes until golden and tender.

🕐 **40 minutes**

✳ Serve with roasted, grilled (broiled) or cold meats or as a vegetarian supper.

# Marrakesh Couscous

**Serves 2**

15 g/½ oz/1 tbsp butter or margarine
1 small onion, diced
2.5 ml/½ tsp ground cinnamon
2.5 ml/½ tsp ground coriander (cilantro)
100 g/4 oz couscous
100 ml/3½ fl oz/scant ½ cup vegetable stock
50 g/2 oz/½ cup raisins
50 g/2 oz/½ cup flaked (slivered) almonds, toasted
15 ml/1 tbsp chopped coriander
Salt and freshly ground black pepper

1  Heat the butter or margarine in a saucepan, add the onion and cook for 2 minutes until softened.

2  Add the cinnamon and ground coriander, stir in the couscous and stock and bring to the boil. Remove from the heat, cover and leave to stand for 5 minutes.

3  Fluff up the couscous with a fork and stir in the raisins, almonds and chopped coriander. Season to taste.

🕐 *20 minutes*

✹  Serve this as a light supper dish or with Kasbah Lamb with Apricots (page 64).

# Spiced Thai Noodles

**Serves 2**
175 g/6 oz dried egg noodles
25 g/1 oz creamed coconut
175 ml/6 fl oz/¾ cup hot water
15 ml/1 tbsp red or green Thai curry paste
5 ml/1 tsp lemon grass purée (paste)
30 ml/2 tbsp chopped coriander (cilantro)
Salt and freshly ground black pepper

1 Cook the noodles according to the packet directions.

2 Place the creamed coconut and water in a bowl and mix until smooth.

3 Add all the remaining ingredients, seasoning to taste with salt and pepper and serve immediately.

🕓 15 minutes

✶ This is a good accompaniment to spicy oriental kebabs or grilled (broiled) meats.

# Pilau Rice with Bacon

### Serves 2

15 g/½ oz/1 tbsp butter or margarine
100 g/4 oz/½ cup wild rice mix
250 ml/8 fl oz/1 cup chicken stock
100 g/4 oz canned sweetcorn (corn) and pimiento, drained
2 small courgettes (zucchini), diced
Salt and freshly ground black pepper
6 smoked bacon rashers (slices), grilled (broiled)
25 g/1 oz/¼ cup pine nuts, toasted
Chopped parsley, to garnish

1 Melt the butter or margarine in a pan, add the rice and fry (sauté), tossing well, for 2–3 minutes until turning opaque.

2 Add the stock, cover and simmer gently for 15 minutes until nearly all the liquid is absorbed.

3 Add the sweetcorn and pimiento, courgettes and salt and pepper. Stir and heat for a further 5 minutes.

4 Serve topped with the bacon and garnished with the pine nuts and parsley.

### 🕐 25 minutes

✳ You can substitute vegetarian rashers for the bacon if you prefer.

# Roasted Vegetable Ciabatta

**Serves 2**

½ red (bell) pepper, seeded and quartered
½ green pepper, seeded and quartered
½ yellow pepper, seeded and quartered
2 small red onions, peeled and quartered
30 ml/2 tbsp olive oil
1 small ciabatta loaf, thickly sliced
75 g/3 oz/¾ cup Feta cheese, finely diced
Green and black olives, stoned (pitted)

1 Spread out the peppers and onions on a roasting tray and drizzle with the oil. Roast in a preheated oven at 200°C/400°F/gas mark 6 for 15 minutes.

2 Lay the peppers and onions on the ciabatta slices.

3 Sprinkle with the cheese and olives and serve warm as a snack or supper dish.

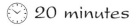 20 minutes

# Bacon and Parmesan Granary Wedges

**Serves 2**

100 g/4 oz/1 cup granary flour
10 ml/2 tsp baking powder
1.5 ml/¼ tsp cayenne
A pinch of salt
25 g/1 oz/2 tbsp butter or margarine
2 back bacon rashers (slices), cooked and finely chopped
15 ml/1 tbsp grated Parmesan cheese
75 ml/5 tbsp milk

1 Place the flour, baking powder, cayenne and salt in a bowl. Rub in the butter or margarine until the mixture resembles fine breadcrumbs.

2 Add the bacon and Parmesan and mix well.

3 Add enough of the milk to form a soft dough. Knead lightly and roll into a 2.5 cm/1 in thick round. Cut into four wedges and place on a baking (cookie) sheet.

4 Brush with milk and bake in a preheated oven at 220°C/425°F/gas mark 7 for 10 minutes until risen and golden brown. Allow to cool before serving.

🕐 *20 minutes*

✳ Serve the wedges with a cheese board and pickles or a vegetable salad. Vegetarians can use vegetarian rashers instead of bacon.

# Speedy Milano Salami and Tuna Pizza

## Serves 2

75 g/3 oz sun-dried tomato purée (paste)
A 25 cm/10 in thin and crispy pizza base
50 g/2 oz mini salami slices
90 g/3½ oz/1 small can of tuna chunks or flakes in brine, drained
75 g/3 oz/¾ cup Dolcelatte cheese, crumbled
Freshly ground black pepper
Crisp green salad, to serve

1 Spread the tomato purée evenly over the pizza base and arrange the salami slices on top.

2 Scatter with the tuna and cheese and add a sprinkling of pepper.

3 Bake directly on the top shelf of a preheated oven at 220°C/425°F/gas mark 7 for 10–12 minutes until golden brown and bubbling. (Place a baking tray under the cooking shelf to catch any falling juices.)

4 Serve hot or cold with a crisp green salad.

## ⏲ 15 minutes

✶ For a variation, use Stilton or Mozzarella cheese instead of Dolcelatte cheese and add a sprinkling of chopped capers, olives or anchovy fillets.

# Griddled Polenta Popovers

**Serves 2**

250 g/9 oz/1 block of prepared polenta, cut into 8 slices
30 ml/2 tbsp sun-dried tomato purée (paste)
25 g/1 oz/¼ cup Parmesan cheese, grated
8 sun-blush tomatoes, sliced
15 ml/1 tbsp shredded basil leaves
15 ml/1 tbsp olive oil

1 Spread half the polenta slices with the tomato purée. Sprinkle with the Parmesan and top with the tomatoes and basil.

2 Place a polenta slice on top and brush both sides with the oil.

3 Cook on a griddle or in a frying pan (skillet) for 3–4 minutes each side, then serve immediately.

🕐 **10 minutes**

✳ For a variation, substitute green pesto for the sun-dried tomato purée, or use my nut-free pesto on page 13.

# Peperoni Baked Eggs

## Serves 2

75 g/3 oz peperoni, sliced
10 ml/2 tsp olive oil
1 small red onion, thinly sliced
7.5 ml/1½ tsp sun-dried tomato purée
2.5 ml/½ tsp dried mixed herbs
200 g/7 oz/1 small can of chopped tomatoes with garlic
75 g/3 oz/1 small tub of mixed peppers in tomato dressing
2 large eggs
Freshly ground black pepper
Warm crusty bread, to serve

1   Roughly chop 25 g/1 oz of the peperoni.

2   Heat the oil and fry (sauté) the onion for 2 minutes.

3   Stir in the tomato purée, herbs, tomatoes and peppers. Add the chopped peperoni and mix well. Cook for 2 minutes.

4   Divide the mixture between 2 ovenproof dishes and break an egg into the centre of each. Arrange the remaining peperoni around the edge and sprinkle with pepper.

5   Bake in a preheated oven at 200°C/400°F/gas mark 6 for 10–15 minutes until the eggs are set.

6   Serve with warm crusty bread.

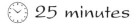 25 minutes

# Ham Ciabatta Toasts

**Serves 2**

2 tomatoes, chopped
50 g/2 oz/½ cup ham, chopped
50 g/2 oz/½ cup Mozzarella cheese, chopped
6 black olives, stoned (pitted) and roughly chopped
10 ml/2 tsp chopped basil
Freshly ground black pepper
1 small ciabatta loaf, cut into 8 slices
30 ml/2 tbsp red or green pesto sauce

1   Place the tomatoes, ham, cheese, olives and basil in a bowl. Season with pepper and mix well to combine.

2   Spread the ciabatta slices with the pesto and top with the ham mixture.

3   Place under a hot grill (broiler) for 3–4 minutes until golden brown and serve immediately.

🕐 **10 minutes**

✶  For a nut-free pesto, see page 13.

# Mozzarella and Egg Potato Nests

**Serves 2**

10 ml/2 tsp sunflower oil
1 small onion, peeled and finely chopped
350 g/12 oz potatoes, cooked and mashed
30 ml/2 tbsp milk
Salt and freshly ground pepper
2 eggs
25 g/1 oz/¼ cup Mozzarella cheese, grated

1 Heat the oil and fry (sauté) the onion for 2 minutes.

2 Stir in the potatoes with the milk and seasoning.

3 Transfer to a greased oval dish and smooth the top. Form two shallow wells in the potato and break an egg into each.

4 Sprinkle the cheese over the top and bake in a preheated oven at 180°C/350°F/gas mark 4 for 15–20 minutes until the potatoes are golden and the eggs are set.

### 🕐 25 minutes

✶ To make this a more substantial dish, add chopped mushrooms or diced cooked bacon to the mashed potato.

# Roasted Vegetable and Feta Crisps

**Serves 2**

150 g/5 oz shortcrust pastry (basic pie crust), thawed if frozen
1 small aubergine (eggplant), cubed
1 red, green or yellow (bell) pepper, seeded
and cut into chunks
2 small courgettes (zucchini), sliced
1 red onion, peeled and cut into wedges
15 ml/1 tbsp olive oil
Salt and freshly ground black pepper
75 g/3 oz/¾ cup Feta cheese, broken into pieces
Crisp green salad, to serve

1   Halve the pastry (paste) and roll each piece into a 13 cm/ 5 in round. Place on a baking (cookie) sheet.

2   Place the vegetables in a roasting tin (pan) and add the oil and seasoning. Toss well to coat. Roast in a preheated oven at 220°C/425°F/gas mark 7 for 20 minutes, tossing once during cooking.

3   Remove from oven and spoon over the pastry bases. Scatter the cheese on top, then return to the oven and bake for a further 10 minutes until the cheese and vegetables are golden and the pastry is cooked.

4   Serve immediately with a crisp green salad.

⏱ **40 minutes**

✴ For a variation, substitute goats' cheese for the Feta. This could also be served as a starter in small pastry cases (pie shells).

# Pesto Garlic Bread

**Serves 2**

100 g/4 oz/½ cup butter or margarine, softened
5 ml/1 tsp garlic purée (paste)
45 ml/3 tbsp green pesto sauce
1 small French stick, cut into 8 slices
50 g/2 oz/½ cup Parmesan cheese, grated

1   Mix together the butter or margarine, garlic purée and pesto.

2   Grill (broil) the bread lightly on both sides. Spread the pesto butter over one side and grill again until melted.

3   Sprinkle the Parmesan over the top while still hot and serve immediately.

🕐 10 minutes

✻   For a nut-free pesto, see page 13.

# Sandwich Fillings

These ingredients will fill two sandwiches and all take less than 10 minutes to prepare. Instead of using four slices of bread, you could use two large flour tortillas, folded round the filling or rolled up and sliced.

## Tuna and Pepper

75 g/3 oz tuna chunks in oil, drained and flaked
15 ml/1 tbsp mayonnaise
15 ml/1 tbsp fromage frais
¼ red, green or yellow (bell) pepper, finely chopped
Salt and black pepper
2 large pitta breads
Butter or margarine, for spreading
4 iceberg lettuce leaves

1　Mix together the tuna, mayonnaise, fromage frais and chopped pepper and season to taste.

2　Warm the pitta breads and split them to form pockets. When cool, spread with the butter or margarine, place a lettuce leaf in the bottom of each and top with the tuna filling.

## Chocolate and Banana

60 ml/4 tbsp chocolate and vanilla spread
2 small bananas, thinly sliced

1　Spread two slices of bread with the spread and scatter the banana slices over. Top with the remaining slices of bread.

# Cottage Top

30 ml/2 tbsp peanut butter
50 g/2 oz wafer-thin ham slices
60 ml/4 tbsp cottage cheese

1   Spread two slices of bread with the peanut butter, then add the ham and finally the cottage cheese. Top with the remaining slices of bread.

# Honey and Apple

2 small eating (dessert) apples
A little lemon juice
60 ml/4 tbsp set honey
2.5 ml/½ tsp grated nutmeg or ground cinnamon

1   Peel the apples, grate them and toss in the lemon juice to prevent browning.

2   Spread two slices of bread with the honey, place the apple on top and sprinkle with the spice. Top with the remaining slices of bread.

# Peanut Butter and Ham

60 ml/4 tbsp crunchy peanut butter
50 g/2 oz wafer thin ham slices
1 large carrot, grated

1   Spread two slices of bread with the peanut butter, place the ham on top and sprinkle with the carrot. Top with the remaining slices of bread.

# Dips

## Watercress Dip
**Serves 2**

25 g/1 oz watercress
75 ml/5 tbsp Greek-style yoghurt
2 spring onions (scallions)
Salt and black pepper

1   Place all the ingredients in a food processor and mix until smooth.

2   Chill before serving.

🕐 5 minutes

✳ Serve with grilled (broiled) or battered fish and seafood.

## Corn and Tomato Salsa
**Serves 2**

30 ml/2 tbsp sweetcorn (corn), cooked
5 cm/2 in piece of cucumber, finely diced
4 cherry tomatoes, diced
60 ml/4 tbsp tomato ketchup (catsup)
Freshly ground black pepper
Tabasco sauce (optional)

1   Mix together all the ingredients, adding Tabasco sauce to taste, if wished.

🕐 5 minutes

✳ Serve with tortillas or breaded cod fillets.

# Creamy Korma Dip

**Serves 2**

100 ml/3½ fl oz/scant ½ cup crème fraîche
15 ml/1 tbsp korma curry paste
30 ml/2 tbsp mango chutney
A squeeze of lemon or lime juice
15 ml/1 tbsp sultanas (golden raisins) (optional)

1   Place all the ingredients in a bowl and mix until combined.

### ⏱ 5 minutes

✳ Serve this dip with bread sticks, crudités or cherry tomatoes, or use it as a topping for jacket potatoes.

# Cucumber and Mint Raita

**Serves 2**

150 ml/¼ pt/⅔ cup plain yoghurt
2.5 cm/1 in piece of cucumber, finely diced
15 ml/1 tbsp mint, finely chopped
2.5 ml/½ tsp crushed garlic

1   Mix together all the ingredients and chill.

### ⏱ 5 minutes

✳ Serve as an accompaniment to curries, onion bhajis, pitta breads or naan bread.

# Ciabatta Special

**Serves 2**

30 ml/2 tbsp mayonnaise
15 ml/1 tbsp roughly chopped chives
Salt and freshly ground black pepper
1 small ciabatta loaf, halved and sliced horizontally
3 plum tomatoes, sliced
1 small avocado, stoned (pitted), peeled and sliced
4 slices of blue Rosenborg cheese

1  Place the mayonnaise, chives and salt and pepper in a bowl and mix to combine. Spread over the bottom slices of the ciabatta.

2  Arrange the tomato and avocado slices on the mayonnaise mixture and top with the cheese.

3  Put the remaining ciabatta slices on top and serve.

### ⏱ 10 minutes

✷  If you cannot get Rosenborg cheese you can use another Swiss cheese such as Emmental instead.

# Salads

The best thing about salads is that they are so quick and easy to prepare, but they are also unbeatable value and can be served for lunch or supper. Don't worry if you don't have all the ingredients for the recipe; as long as the flavours complement each other you can make any imaginative substitutions.

# Roasted Pesto Vegetable Salad with Goats' Cheese

**Serves 2**

1 small red (bell) pepper, seeded and cut into wedges
1 small yellow pepper, seeded and cut into wedges
2 small courgettes (zucchini), diagonally sliced
8 chestnut mushrooms, halved
1 red onion, cut into wedges
45 ml/3 tbsp green pesto sauce
Freshly ground black pepper
75 g/3 oz goats' cheese, thinly sliced
15 ml/1 tbsp pine nuts, toasted
5 ml/1 tsp rosemary leaves

1   Place the vegetables in a bowl, add the pesto and toss well. Chill and leave to marinade for 1 hour.

2   Transfer to a baking tin (pan), season with pepper and roast in a preheated oven at 200°C/400°F/gas mark 6 for 20 minutes, tossing halfway through the cooking time.

3   Transfer to a warm serving dish, top with the slices of cheese and sprinkle with the pine nuts and rosemary to garnish.

🕐 *30 minutes, plus marinating*

✱   Serve with roast chicken or lamb cutlets. For a nut-free pesto, see page 13.

# Carrot and Apple Salad

**Serves 2**

2 small red eating (dessert) apples
A little lemon juice
175 g/6 oz carrots, peeled and coarsely grated
15 ml/1 tbsp raisins or sultanas (golden raisins)
15 ml/1 tbsp sunflower seeds
45 ml/3 tbsp salad dressing
Mixed lettuce leaves, to serve

1   Peel, core and slice the apples, then toss them in the lemon juice to prevent browning.

2   Place the carrots, apples, raisins or sultanas and sunflower seeds in a bowl and toss well to combine.

3   Pour the dressing over, toss again and serve on a bed of mixed salad leaves.

🕧 10 minutes

✴ This salad tastes good with cold meats and new potatoes.

# Quick Caesar Salad

**Serves 2**

1 small hard-boiled (hard-cooked) egg, chopped
2.5 ml/½ tsp Dijon mustard
5 ml/1 tsp Worcestershire sauce
2.5 ml/½ tsp crushed garlic
A squeeze of lime juice
Salt and freshly ground black pepper
60 ml/4 tbsp olive oil
1 small cos lettuce, washed and dried
30 ml/2 tbsp cooked lardons or cubed bacon
60 ml/4 tbsp garlic croûtons
25 g/1 oz/¼ cup Parmesan cheese, coarsely grated

1  Place the egg, mustard, Worcestershire sauce, garlic, lime juice and salt and pepper in a food blender and process until smooth.

2  With the machine running, gradually add the oil until the dressing is smooth and thick.

3  Tear the lettuce into large pieces and place in a shallow bowl. Spoon the dressing over and toss well.

4  Scatter the lardons, croûtons and Parmesan over and serve immediately.

⏲ **10 minutes**

✳ If you do not have a food blender, mash the egg with the other ingredients, then gradually whisk in the oil until you have a smooth dressing. For a more authentic Caesar salad, you can substitute 4 chopped anchovy fillets for the bacon pieces.

# Mushroom and Mangetout Salad

**Serves 2**

4 spring onions (scallions), sliced
100 g/4 oz chestnut mushrooms, sliced
60 ml/4 tbsp plain yoghurt
Salt and freshly ground black pepper
100 g/4 oz mangetout (snow peas), cooked, drained and cooled
Chopped parsley, to garnish

1 Place the spring onions and mushrooms in a bowl and toss together. Add the yoghurt, season to taste and mix together carefully.

2 Arrange the mangetout on a serving plate. Top with the mushroom mixture and garnish with parsley. Serve chilled.

🕐 5 minutes, plus chilling

# New Potato and Chickpea Salad

**Serves 2**

15 ml/1 tbsp mayonnaise
30 ml/2 tbsp fromage frais
10 ml/2 tsp snipped chives
2.5 ml/½ tsp red or green chilli, finely chopped
A squeeze of lemon juice
Salt and freshly ground black pepper
225 g/8 oz baby new potatoes, cooked
100 g/4 oz canned chickpeas (garbanzos)

1   Mix together the mayonnaise, fromage frais, chives, chilli,
    lemon juice and salt and pepper to taste.

2   Add the potatoes and chickpeas and toss well to coat.

### 🕐 5 minutes

✳   Serve as an accompaniment to salads and grilled (broiled)
    or barbecued meats. For a variation, you can omit the
    chives and use another of your favourite herbs.

# Pasta Niçoise

**Serves 2**

75 g/3 oz pasta shells, cooked
75 g/3 oz canned sweetcorn (corn), drained
75 g/3 oz canned kidney beans, drained
75 g/3 oz cherry tomatoes, halved
100 g/4 oz tuna chunks, drained and flaked
4 spring onions (scallions), sliced
45 ml/3 tbsp olive oil
30 ml/2 tbsp white wine vinegar
10 ml/2 tsp Dijon mustard
Salt and freshly ground black pepper
2 hard-boiled (hard-cooked) eggs, quartered
25 g/1 oz anchovy fillets, drained
10 ml/2 tsp chopped parsley
Granary bread, to serve

1  Place the pasta, sweetcorn, kidney beans, tomatoes, tuna and spring onions in a bowl.

2  Whisk together the oil, wine vinegar, mustard and salt and pepper, pour over the salad and toss gently.

3  Arrange the eggs and anchovies on top and sprinkle with the parsley. Serve with granary bread.

 5 minutes

# Prawn and Pepper Salad

**Serves 2**

175g/6 oz cooked, peeled prawns (shrimp)
A squeeze of lemon juice
2.5 ml/½ tsp paprika
1 small red onion, thinly sliced
2 spring onions (scallions), thinly sliced
1 small red (bell) pepper, seeded and thinly sliced
100 g/4 oz baby new potatoes, cooked and halved
8 black or green olives, halved and stoned (pitted)
5 ml/1 tsp chopped parsley
15 ml/1 tbsp Thousand Island dressing
50 g/2 oz/1 bag of Italian-style salad
2 hard-boiled (hard-cooked) eggs, quartered
Lemon wedges, to garnish
Crusty bread, to serve

1 Place the prawns in a bowl and toss with the lemon juice and paprika.

2 Place the onion, spring onions, red pepper, potatoes, olives and parsley in a separate bowl and toss well.

3 Add the prawn mixture and dressing and mix carefully to coat.

4 Line a serving bowl with the salad leaves and spoon the prawn mixture on top.

5 Garnish with the eggs and lemon wedges and serve with fresh crusty bread.

 5 minutes

# Provençal Salad

**Serves 2**
60 ml/4 tbsp water
15 ml/1 tbsp olive oil
30 ml/2 tbsp white wine vinegar
5 ml/1 tsp made mustard
1 garlic clove, crushed
15 ml/1 tbsp herbes de Provence
Salt and freshly ground black pepper
100 g/4 oz French (green) beans, trimmed and cooked
225 g/8 oz waxy potatoes, cooked and sliced
1 courgette (zucchini), diced
1 red or yellow (bell) pepper, seeded and diced
1 red onion, chopped
12 black olives
1 small bunch of basil
1 small head of radicchio, cut into bite-sized pieces
Crusty bread, to serve

1 Place the water, oil, wine vinegar, mustard, garlic, herbs and salt and pepper in a bowl or screw-topped jar and whisk or shake well to combine.

2 Slice the beans into 2.5 cm/1 in lengths and place in a bowl with the potatoes, courgette, diced pepper, onion and olives. Toss thoroughly.

3 Pour the dressing over, toss again and chill.

4 Discard the stalks from the basil and tear the leaves roughly.

5 Just before serving, add the radicchio and basil to the salad and toss well. Serve with crusty bread.

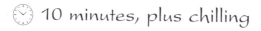 10 minutes, plus chilling

# Salmon and Goats' Cheese Salad

**Serves 2**

1 small ripe avocado, stoned (pitted), peeled and diced
Juice of ½ lime
15 ml/1 tbsp olive oil
15 ml/1 tbsp balsamic vinegar
7.5 ml/1½ tsp soft brown sugar
7.5 ml/1½ tsp sun-dried tomato purée (paste)
Freshly ground black pepper
50 g/2 oz/1 bag of baby leaf salad
4 slices of smoked salmon, cut into strips
50 g/2 oz/½ cup goats' cheese, diced
5 cm/2 in piece of cucumber, peeled and diced
8 cherry tomatoes, halved
12 black olives
Crusty bread, to serve

1   Toss the avocado in the lime juice to prevent browning.

2   Place the oil, vinegar, sugar, tomato purée and pepper in a bowl or screw-topped jar and whisk or shake well to combine.

3   Lay the salad leaves on a serving plate and arrange the avocado, salmon, cheese, cucumber, tomatoes and olives on top.

4   Pour the dressing over the salad and serve immediately with fresh crusty bread.

## ⌚ 10 minutes

✶  Feta cheese can be used instead of goats' cheese.

# Tomato, Olive and Mozzarella Salad

**Serves 2**

2 beefsteak tomatoes, sliced
100 g/4 oz Mozzarella cheese, sliced
A small handful of basil leaves
8 green olives, stoned (pitted) and halved across the centre
8 black olives, stoned and halved across the centre
30 ml/2 tbsp olive oil
Freshly ground black pepper

1 Layer alternate slices of tomato and Mozzarella on a serving plate. Scatter the basil and olives over the top.

2 Drizzle with the oil and season with black pepper. Serve immediately.

### 5 minutes

✶ You could also arrange a small handful of rocket leaves on the serving plate and use them as a base for the salad.

# Tuna and Rice Medley Salad

**Serves 2**

75 g/3 oz/⅓ cup brown rice, cooked
45 ml/3 tbsp vinaigrette dressing
1 small red (bell) pepper, seeded and diced
4 spring onions (scallions), diagonally sliced
5 cm/2 in piece of cucumber, diced
50 g/2 oz sweetcorn (corn), cooked
50 g/2 oz canned kidney beans
2 celery sticks, diced
25 g/1 oz/¼ cup cashew nuts, halved
Salt and freshly ground black pepper
200 g/7 oz/1 small can of tuna in brine, drained and flaked
Continental bread, to serve

1  Place the rice in a bowl, add the vinaigrette and toss well.

2  Add all the remaining ingredients except the tuna and mix to combine.

3  Carefully spoon in the tuna. Chill.

4  Serve with continental bread.

⏱ 5 minutes, plus chilling

✸ Sliced ham, chicken or goats' cheese make great alternatives to the tuna.

# Tuna and Spinach Salad

**Serves 2**

15 ml/1 tbsp olive oil
2 tuna steaks
1 small red onion, finely sliced
12 cherry tomatoes
50 g/2 oz spinach leaves, torn into pieces
Freshly ground black pepper
1 lemon, cut into wedges
5 ml/1 tsp balsamic vinegar
Crusty bread, to serve

1 Heat half the olive oil in a pan and cook the tuna for 4–5 minutes, turning once. Remove from the pan and break into bite-sized pieces.

2 Add the remaining oil and cook the onion for 2–3 minutes. Add the tomatoes and cook for 1 minute.

3 Stir in the spinach and return the tuna to the pan and cook for 1 minute.

4 Season with pepper, the juice from one of the lemon wedges and the vinegar.

5 Place in a salad bowl with the juices and garnish with the remaining lemon wedges. Serve with crusty bread.

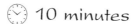 10 minutes

# Waldorf Turkey Salad with Fruited Dressing

**Serves 2**

1 small red eating (dessert) apple, unpeeled
A squeeze of lemon juice
225 g/8 oz/2 cups cooked turkey, diced
50 g/2 oz seedless black grapes, halved
2 celery sticks, sliced
45 ml/3 tbsp mayonnaise
30 ml/2 tbsp peach or mango chutney
Salt and freshly ground black pepper
25 g/1 oz/¼ cup cashew nuts, halved
Watercress, to garnish
Cold cooked rice, tossed in a vinaigrette dressing,
and cherry tomatoes, to serve

1 Core and slice the apple and toss in the lemon juice to prevent browning.

2 Add the turkey, grapes and celery. Toss again to combine.

3 Blend the mayonnaise with the chutney and add to the meat mixture. Fold in to coat the ingredients and season with salt and pepper.

4 Spoon into a serving dish and garnish with the nuts and watercress.

5 Serve with rice in a vinaigrette dressing and cherry tomatoes.

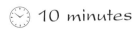 10 minutes

# Warm Potato and Dolcelatte Salad

**Serves 2**
30 ml/2 tbsp olive oil
225 g/8 oz baby new potatoes, washed
Salt and freshly ground black pepper
50g/2 oz/½ cup Dolcelatte cheese, diced
1 small bunch of watercress, trimmed
6 cherry tomatoes, halved
15 ml/1 tbsp balsamic vinegar

1 Heat the oil in a pan, add the potatoes and cook for 15–20 minutes, tossing well, until golden brown and tender. Season with salt and pepper.

2 Add the cheese to the pan and heat until it is just beginning to soften. Season with salt and pepper.

3 Arrange the watercress on two plates, scatter the tomatoes on top and spoon the potato mixture over.

4 Drizzle with the vinegar and serve.

## 🕑 25 minutes

✻ This makes a great starter on its own, or you can serve it as a side dish with hot or cold meats.

# Vine Tomato and Herb Salad

**Serves 2**
45 ml/3 tbsp olive oil
15 ml/1 tbsp white wine vinegar
1 garlic clove, crushed
A squeeze of lemon juice
Salt and freshly ground black pepper
225 g/8 oz vine tomatoes, quartered
15 ml/1 tbsp chopped basil
15 ml/1 tbsp snipped chives
15 g/½ oz/2 tbsp pine nuts, toasted

1 Place the oil, wine vinegar, garlic, lemon juice and salt and pepper in a bowl or screw-topped jar and whisk or shake well to combine.

2 Place the tomatoes in a bowl. Add the basil and chives and toss well. Pour the dressing over and chill.

3 Sprinkle with the pine nuts just before serving.

 5 minutes

# Desserts

For many people the dessert is the eagerly awaited finishing touch to any meal. Many can be made with no cooking at all and, by using some ready-prepared ingredients, the task of assembling a recipe is cut to the minimum and leaves hardly any washing up.

# Apricot and Ricotta Strudel

### Serves 2

425 g/15 oz/1 large can of apricot halves in
natural juice, drained
50 g/2 oz/¼ cup ricotta cheese
2 sheets of filo pastry (paste)
15 ml/1 tbsp melted butter or margarine
25 g/1 oz/¼ cup ground almonds
Milk, for glazing
Icing (confectioners') sugar, for dusting
Single (light) or double (heavy) cream, to serve

1  Place the apricots and ricotta in a bowl and mix together.

2  Cut the pastry sheets in half along the longest length. Lay
two sheets on top of each other and brush with the butter
or margarine. Sprinkle with the almonds and lay the
remaining two sheets on top.

3  Spoon the apricot mixture along one short edge of the
pastry to within 2 cm/¾ in of each side. Fold in the edges to
enclose the filling and roll up to form a small sausage
shape.

4  Place on a baking tray, brush with milk and bake in the
centre of a preheated oven at 180°C/350°F/gas mark 4 for
25–30 minutes until golden brown.

5  Dust with icing sugar and serve with cream.

 45 minutes

# Baked Peach Dream

### Serves 2

15 g/½ oz/1 tbsp butter or margarine
2 peaches, halved and stoned (pitted)
30 ml/2 tbsp soft brown sugar
30 ml/2 tbsp white wine
5 ml/1 tsp grated lime rind
15 ml/1 tbsp lime juice
10 ml/2 tsp clear honey
25 g/1 oz/¼ cup pistachio nuts, roughly chopped
100 g/4 oz/½ cup Mascarpone cheese

1  Grease a shallow ovenproof dish with the butter or margarine. Arrange the peach halves, cut-side up, in the dish.

2  Place the sugar in the centre of each and pour half the wine over.

3  Bake in a preheated oven at 180°C/350°F/gas mark 4 for 15–20 minutes until tender.

4  Mix together the remaining wine, the lime rind, lime juice, honey, nuts and Mascarpone cheese.

5  Transfer the peach halves to individual plates and serve with the pistachio cream.

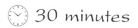 30 minutes

# Baked Tropical Fruit with Lime Chocolate Sauce

**Serves 2**

15 g/½ oz/1 tbsp butter or margarine
Fruit of your choice such as fresh pineapple or mango cubes, halved strawberries or apricots, sliced peaches, quartered plums, banana chunks
Grated rind and juice of ½ lime
75 g/3 oz/¾ cup white chocolate

1 Grease two squares of foil large enough to wrap the fruit with the butter or margarine.

2 Lay the fruits in the centre of each and sprinkle with half the lime juice. Gather up the foil to form a parcel.

3 Place on a baking (cookie) sheet and cook in a preheated oven at 200°C/400°F/gas mark 6 for 5–6 minutes.

4 Place the chocolate and remaining lime juice in a bowl set over a pan of hot water. Heat, stirring, until the chocolate has melted and the mixture is smooth. Add the lime rind.

5 Transfer the fruit to individual dishes and top with the lime chocolate sauce.

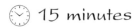 15 minutes

# Black Cherry Clafoutis

**Serves 2**

225 g/8 oz ripe black cherries
*For the batter:*
40 g/1½ oz plain (all-purpose) flour
15 g/½ oz/1 tbsp caster (superfine) sugar
2 small eggs
100 ml/3½ fl oz/scant ½ cup milk
A few drops of vanilla essence (extract)
Butter or margarine, for greasing
Icing (confectioners') sugar, for dusting
Single (light) or double (heavy) cream, to serve

1   Remove the stones (pits) from the cherries over a bowl to catch any juices. Add the cherry flesh to the bowl.

2   Blend together the batter ingredients.

3   Grease a 750 ml/1¼ pt/3 cup soufflé dish with the butter or margarine. Heat for a few minutes in a preheated oven at 200°C/400°F/gas mark 6.

4   Add the cherries and juice. Cover with the batter and bake for 20–25 minutes until well risen.

5   Dust with icing sugar and serve immediately with cream.

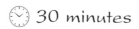 30 minutes

# Caramel and Orange Tortilla Layer

## Serves 2

100 g/4 oz/½ cup caster (superfine) sugar
45 ml/3 tbsp double (heavy) cream
25 g/1 oz/¼ cup unsalted cashew nuts, halved
1 large orange, peeled and segmented
20 ml/4 tsp orange liqueur (optional)
2 large flour tortillas
Single (light) or double (heavy) cream, to serve

1   Place the sugar in a pan and heat gently for 2–3 minutes until melted and a golden caramel colour.

2   Stir in the cream and cashew nuts. Remove from the heat and gently fold in the orange segments and liqueur, if using.

3   Using a straight-sided cutter, cut out six 7.5 cm/3 in rounds from each tortilla.

4   Arrange three mini tortilla rounds on each of two plates and top with the orange mixture. Repeat the layers.

5   Serve with cream.

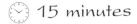 15 minutes

# Whisky and Apple Bread and Butter Pudding

### Serves 2

75 g/3 oz dry crusty French bread, cubed
2 small red eating (dessert) apples, cored and diced
25 g/1 oz/3 tbsp raisins
30 ml/2 tbsp whisky
200 ml/7 fl oz/scant 1 cup milk
2 eggs
50 g/2 oz/¼ cup caster (superfine) sugar
Butter or margarine, for greasing
Single (light) or double (heavy) cream, to serve

1   Place the bread, apples and raisins in a bowl. Pour the whisky and half the milk over and leave to soak for 3–5 minutes until the liquid has been absorbed.

2   Whisk the eggs and sugar together, then slowly whisk in the remaining milk.

3   Grease two ramekins (custard cups) with the butter or margarine and divide the bread mixture between them.

4   Pour the egg mixture over and bake in a preheated oven at 190°C/375°F/gas mark 5 for 25–30 minutes until set and golden brown.

5   Serve warm with cream.

 40 minutes

# Marshmallow and Fruit Kebabs with Chocolate and Honey Dip

### Serves 2

A selection of 3 fruits such as satsuma, banana, pear, kiwi
fruit, peach, nectarine, apricot, apple
30 ml/2 tbsp lemon juice
12 pink and white marshmallows
*For the chocolate and honey dip:*
50 g/2 oz/½ cup good-quality plain (semi-sweet) chocolate
120 ml/4 fl oz/½ cup crème fraîche
20 ml/4 tsp clear honey

1  Prepare the fruit and cut it into chunks or thick slices.
   Sprinkle with the lemon juice to prevent browning.

2  Thread the fruit pieces and marshmallows alternately on to
   skewers.

3  To make the dip, melt the chocolate in a bowl set over a
   pan of gently simmering water and gently warm the crème
   fraîche in a separate bowl over hot water until softened.

4  Mix the chocolate and crème fraîche together, then stir in
   the honey.

5   Serve the kebabs with the dip.

### 15 minutes

✶  You need a really sweet tooth for this delicious dip, or you may prefer to serve the kebabs with fromage frais or a fruit purée. You can also serve the dip with any fresh fruits or use it as a topping for ice cream.

# Banana and Honey Fool

**Serves 2**

60 ml/4 tbsp clear honey
2 small bananas
5 ml/1 tsp lemon juice
200 g/7 oz ready-to-serve custard
100 g/4 oz fromage frais
25 ml/1½ tbsp soft brown sugar
5 ml/1 tsp chopped nuts

1   Place half the honey in the bottom of two glasses or sundae dishes.

2   Mash 1½ of the bananas with the lemon juice. Add the custard, fromage frais and sugar. Stir until combined and pour over the honey.

3   Slice the remaining banana, layer on top of the fool and pour the remaining honey over.

4   Sprinkle with the nuts and serve.

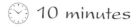 10 minutes

# Chocolate Refrigerator Slices

**Serves 2**

50 g/2 oz digestive biscuits (graham crackers), roughly broken
40 g/1½ oz/¼ cup no-need-to-soak dried apricots,
finely chopped
25 g/1 oz/3 tbsp raisins
15 g/½ oz/2 tbsp pine nuts, chopped
75 g/3 oz/¾ cup milk (sweet) chocolate
25 g/1 oz/2 tbsp butter or margarine
Icing (confectioners') sugar or single (light) cream, to serve

1 Place the biscuit pieces, apricots, raisins and pine nuts in a bowl and mix to combine.

2 Melt the chocolate and butter or margarine in a bowl set over a pan of hot water, stirring until smooth. Allow to cool.

3 Pour the chocolate over the biscuit mixture and stir until mixed.

4 Spoon on to a sheet of greaseproof (waxed) paper and wrap the paper around the biscuit mixture to form a sausage shape about 10 cm/4 in long. Chill for about 40 minutes until firm.

5 Cut into four 2.5 cm/1 in slices. Place two on each plate and serve dusted with icing sugar or with cream poured over.

🕐 10 minutes, plus cooling and chilling

✳ You can use chopped dates instead of apricots and walnuts instead of pine nuts, if you prefer.

# Cool Fruit Brûlée

**Serves 2**

100 g/4 oz fresh raspberries
50 g/2 oz seedless green grapes, halved
3 fresh apricots, stoned (pitted) and sliced
30 ml/2 tbsp Greek yoghurt
30 ml/2 tbsp crème fraîche
30 ml/2 tbsp fromage frais
15 ml/1 tbsp soft brown sugar
1.5 ml/¼ tsp ground cinnamon
Wafer biscuits (cookies), to serve

1 Mix the fruits together and divide between two sundae dishes.

2 Mix together the yoghurt, crème fraîche, fromage frais and 10 ml/2 tsp of the sugar. Spoon over the fruit to cover.

3 Mix the remaining sugar with the cinnamon and sprinkle over the top.

4 Serve with crisp wafer biscuits.

🕐 10 minutes, plus chilling (optional)

✴ This recipe can be prepared in advance and chilled or served immediately.

# Peach and Strawberry Melba Meringue

**Serves 2**

100 g/4 oz canned peach slices in fruit juice, drained and
juice reserved
150 g/5 oz ready-to-serve custard
150 ml/¼ pt/⅔ cup peach melba yoghurt
2 meringue nests, roughly crumbled
50 g/2 oz strawberries, halved
Mint sprigs, to serve

1  Purée half the peaches in the reserved juice and chop the remainder.

2  Mix the custard with the yoghurt until smooth.

3  Spoon the peach purée into two glasses or sundae dishes, sprinkle with half the meringue and half the strawberries. Top with the custard mixture.

4  Repeat with remaining meringue, then the strawberries and chopped peaches.

5  Decorate with mint sprigs and serve immediately.

🕐 10 minutes

✱ For a variation, substitute raspberries and pear halves in juice for the strawberries and peaches and use a kiwi fruit yoghurt instead of peach melba.

# Rich Chocolate and Vanilla Mousse

**Serves 2**

2 egg yolks
15 ml/1 tbsp caster (superfine) sugar
50 g/2 oz/½ cup plain (semi-sweet) 70% cocoa
chocolate, grated
15 ml/1 tbsp water
90 ml/6 tbsp crème fraîche
2.5 ml/½ tsp vanilla essence (extract)
1 egg white
Icing (confectioners') sugar, for dusting
Ratafias or langues de chat biscuits (cookies), to serve

1  Place the egg yolks and sugar in a bowl and whisk with an electric whisk or by hand until thick.

2  Reserve 5 ml/1 tsp of the chocolate for decoration and place the remainder in a bowl with the water. Set the bowl over a pan of hot water and stir until the chocolate has melted and the mixture is smooth. Allow to cool slightly.

3  Whisk the chocolate mixture into the egg yolk mixture, then whisk in the crème fraîche and vanilla essence.

4  Whisk the egg white until softly peaking and carefully fold into the chocolate mixture using a metal spoon.

5  Divide the mixture between two glasses or small ramekins (custard cups) and decorate with the reserved chocolate and a dusting of sieved icing sugar.

6  Serve chilled with ratafias or langues de chats.

 10 minutes, plus chilling

# Strawberries in Balsamic Vinegar

### Serves 2

275 g/10 oz strawberries, hulled and halved
40 ml/2½ tbsp caster (superfine) sugar
75 ml/5 tbsp balsamic vinegar
1 small vanilla pod
125 g/5 oz Mascarpone cheese
6 mint leaves, shredded

1 Place the strawberries in a bowl and sprinkle with 30 ml/ 2 tbsp of the sugar, then the vinegar. Toss gently and leave to marinate for 1½–2 hours if possible.

2 Slice the vanilla pod lengthways, remove the seeds and mix them with the cheese. Add the remaining sugar and stir well.

3 Spoon the vanilla Mascarpone into two sundae dishes, scatter with the strawberries and drizzle some of the balsamic juices over.

4 Sprinkle with the mint leaves to decorate and serve immediately.

🕐 10 minutes, plus marinating

✶ Use the discarded vanilla pod to flavour sugar for other recipes.

# Strawberry and Chocolate Crumb Layer

**Serves 2**

150 g/5 oz strawberries, hulled
7.5 ml/1½ tsp caster (superfine) sugar
15 ml/1 tbsp orange juice
60 ml/4 tbsp plain yoghurt
100 g/4 oz quark
50 g/2 oz/½ cup plain (semi-sweet) chocolate, melted
50 g/2 oz digestive biscuits (graham crackers), crushed
2 mint sprigs

1 Reserve two of the strawberries. Quarter the remainder and place in a bowl with the sugar and orange juice.

2 Place the yoghurt and quark in a bowl and whisk in the chocolate until mixed.

3 Divide half the biscuit crumbs between two glasses. Top with the quartered strawberries and spoon or pipe some of the chocolate mixture over the top. Add a layer of the remaining biscuit crumbs, then the remaining chocolate mixture.

4 Slice the reserved strawberries to make a fan and place on top of the chocolate.

5 Decorate each with a sprig of mint. Chill before serving.

🕐 10 minutes, plus chilling

# Nectarine and Ginger Layer

**Serves 2**

1 nectarine, stoned (pitted) and sliced
1 peach, stoned and sliced
2 apricots, stoned and sliced
15 ml/1 tbsp liqueur of your choice
30 ml/2 tbsp water
150 ml/¼ pt/⅔ cup crème fraîche
150 ml/¼ pt/⅔ cup Greek yoghurt
30 ml/2 tbsp soft dark brown sugar
50 g/2 oz gingernut biscuits (cookies), crushed

1  Place the fruit, liqueur and water in a saucepan. Simmer gently for 3–4 minutes until the fruit has softened and the liquid has reduced. Allow to cool.

2  Mix together the crème fraîche and yoghurt. Place a spoonful in the bottom of two tall glasses or sundae dishes. Top with some of the sugar, then some of the biscuit crumbs, then some of the fruit.

3  Repeat the layers until the glasses are filled, finishing with a layer of fruit. Serve chilled.

🕐 10 minutes, plus cooling and chilling

✴ Any combination of red berries, or a mixture of mango and banana, makes a great alternative.

# Whisky Syllabub

**Serves 2**

60 ml/4 tbsp whisky
5 ml/1 tsp lemon juice
300 ml/½ pt/1¼ cups double (heavy) cream
60 ml/4 tbsp clear honey
Shortbread fingers, to serve

1   Place the whisky, lemon juice and cream in a bowl and whisk until the mixture forms soft peaks. Do not overwhip or the cream will curdle.

2   Spoon into glasses or sundae dishes in alternating layers with the honey. Chill.

3   Serve with shortbread fingers.

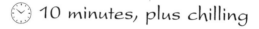 10 minutes, plus chilling

# Tropical Fruit Pancakes

**Serves 2**

4 ready-prepared pancakes or crêpes
60 ml/4 tbsp crème fraîche
100 g/4 oz honeydew melon flesh, cut into small chunks
50 g/2 oz seedless black or green grapes
1 large banana, peeled and sliced
15 ml/1 tbsp soft brown sugar
10 ml/2 tsp lemon juice
Icing (confectioners') sugar, for dusting

1  Spread the pancakes or crêpes with the crème fraîche.

2  Combine the fruits in a bowl and stir in the sugar and lemon juice. Divide the filling between the pancakes, spooning on to a quarter of the base of each. Fold the pancakes into cone shapes.

3  Place the filled pancakes on a serving plate and dust with sieved icing sugar before serving.

🕐 10 minutes

✶ Use fresh pineapple pieces instead of melon for a variation.

# Smoothies and Drinks

This section includes drinks for breakfast, and for hot summer days, refreshing pick-me-ups and winter warmers. They can all be prepared quickly with the minimum of fuss and washing up.

# Breakfast Banana Smoothie

**Serves 2**

2 small bananas, sliced
150 ml/¼ pt/⅔ cup banana and orange yoghurt
20 ml/4 tsp clear honey
175 ml/6 fl oz/¾ cup orange juice
A squeeze of lemon juice

1   Place all the ingredients in a liquidiser or blender and process until smooth. Pour into two glasses and serve chilled.

🕐 5 minutes

✷ This is a good start to the day if you're often too rushed for breakfast, especially as it can be prepared the night before and chilled in the refrigerator.

# Carrot, Orange and Pineapple Refresher

**Serves 2**

2 carrots, peeled and coarsely grated
150 ml/¼ pt/⅔ cup unsweetened orange juice
425 g/15 oz/1 large can of pineapple in natural juice

1   Place all the ingredients in a liquidiser or blender and process until smooth. Pour into two glasses and serve chilled.

🕐 5 minutes

# Mango Smoothie

**Serves 2**

1 small mango, roughly chopped
1 small banana, sliced
150 ml/¼ pt/⅔ cup plain yoghurt
150 ml/¼ pt/⅔ cup milk
30 ml/2 tbsp clear honey
A pinch of ground cinnamon

1 Place the mango, banana, yoghurt, milk and honey in a liquidiser or blender and process until smooth.

2 Pour into glasses and dust each with cinnamon.

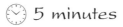 5 minutes

# Tropical Shake

**Serves 2**

50 g/2 oz/⅓ cup ready-to-eat dried apricots, chopped
100 ml/3½ fl oz/scant ½ cup orange juice
100 g/4 oz canned pineapple pieces in natural juice
30 ml/2 tbsp pineapple juice from the can
10 ml/2 tsp honey
2 x 150 ml/2 x 5 fl oz/2 small pots of apricot and mango yoghurt
A pinch of ground cinnamon

1 Place the apricots, orange juice, pineapple pieces and juice, honey and yoghurt in a liquidiser or blender and process until smooth. Pour into two glasses and serve chilled.

5 minutes, plus chilling

# Peach and Banana Smoothie

**Serves 2**

2 peaches, stoned (pitted)
1 banana, sliced
300 ml/½ pt/1¼ cups milk
30 ml/2 tbsp honey
A squeeze of lemon juice
Crushed ice, to serve

1 Place all the ingredients in a liquidiser or blender and process until smooth.

2 Place some crushed ice in two glasses, pour the shake mixture over and serve immediately.

 5 minutes

# Tutti Frutti Smoothie

**Serves 2**

425 g/15 oz evaporated milk, chilled
2 small bananas, sliced
300 ml/½ pt/1¼ cups orange juice, chilled

1 Place all the ingredients in a liquidiser or blender and process until smooth. Pour into two glasses and serve.

 5 minutes

# Strawberry Crush Ice Cream Soda

**Serves 2**

225 g/8 oz strawberries, hulled
2 scoops of vanilla ice cream
300 ml/½ pt/1¼ cups cream soda

1   Place the strawberries in a bowl and crush them roughly.

2   Spoon into the bottom of two glasses and place a scoop of ice cream on top.

3   Pour the cream soda over and serve immediately.

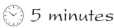 5 minutes

# Coffee Granita

**Serves 2**

60 ml/4 tbsp instant coffee granules
50 g/2 oz/⅓ cup icing (confectioners') sugar
150 ml/¼ pt/⅔ cup boiling water
150 ml/¼ pt/⅔ cup cold water
A few drops of vanilla essence (extract)

1   Dissolve the coffee and icing sugar in the boiling water, then stir in the cold water and vanilla essence. Pour into a shallow container and freeze until ice crystals start to appear.

2   Break down with a fork and pile into two tall glasses.

 5 minutes, plus freezing

# Chocolate Cappuchino Cream

**Serves 2**
400 ml/14 fl oz/1¾ cups milk
50 g/2 oz/½ cup plain (semi-sweet) chocolate
30 ml/2 tbsp whipped cream
Instant coffee powder, to decorate

1 Place the milk and chocolate in a saucepan and heat gently until dissolved.

2 Pour into two glasses, top with the cream and dust with coffee powder.

 5 minutes

# Hot Mocha

**Serves 2**
400 ml/14 fl oz/1¾ cups milk
20 ml/4 tsp drinking chocolate (sweetened chocolate) powder
10 ml/2 tsp instant coffee granules
1 small chocolate flake, crumbled

1 Warm the milk in a saucepan, add the drinking chocolate powder and coffee and stir to dissolve.

2 Pour into two glasses and top with the chocolate pieces.

 5 minutes

# Index

159